THE PASSION IN ART

Jesus was not depicted on the cross until the early fifth century. Since then this scene has been painted or carved in sharply differing ways.

With the aid of over thirty full-page plates, *The Passion in Art* explores the historical contexts and theologies that led to such differing depictions. Because the first Christians saw the Crucifixion and Resurrection of Jesus as different aspects of a unified victory over sin and death, scenes of the Passion are juxtaposed with some of the Resurrection, which again are highly varied in what they do and do not show.

This is the first book to consider the Passion as portrayed in the whole sweep of Christian history. Each picture is considered both from the point of view of its context and its theological standpoint.

Spanning the centuries, the images reproduced and discussed include: scenes from the Passion of Christ in the Catacombs of Domitilla, mosaics in Ravenna, the Rabbula Crucifixion and Resurrection, the Crucifixion Plaque from Metz, the Gero Crucifix, Cimabue's Crucifix, Giotto's *Noli me Tangere*, Piero della Francesca's *Resurrection*, the Isenheim altarpiece, Caravaggio's *Supper at Emmaus*, Rembrandt's *Christ on the Cross*, Chagall's *White Crucifixion*, contemporary paintings by Stanley Spencer, Graham Sutherland, Nicholas Mynheer, and many more works of great acclaim.

For Jo
who has seen many of these works
with me.

THE PASSION IN ART

Richard Harries
Bishop of Oxford

ASHGATE

Published by
Ashgate Publishing Limited
Gower House
Croft Road
Aldershot
Hants GU11 3HR
England

Ashgate Publishing Company
Suite 420
101 Cherry Street
Burlington
Vermont, 05401–4405
USA

Ashgate website: http://www.ashgate.com

British Library Cataloguing in Publication Data
Harries, Richard
    The Passion in Art. – (Ashgate Studies in Theology, Imagination and the Arts) 1. Jesus Christ – Passion – Art. 2. Jesus Christ – Crucifixion – Art. 3. Jesus Christ – Resurrection – Art. 4. Christian art and symbolism. I. Title.
    704.9'4853

US Library of Congress Cataloging in Publication Data
Harries, Richard
    The Passion in Art / Richard Harries.
        p.   cm. – (Ashgate Studies in Theology, Imagination and the Arts)
    Includes bibliographical references and ndex
    1. Jesus Christ – Passion – Art. I. Title. II. Series.
    N8052.4H37 2004
    704.9'4853–dc22

                                                            2003025791

ISBN 0 7546 5010 3 (hbk)
ISBN 0 7546 5011 1 (pbk)

This book is printed on acid free paper.

Typeset by Bournemouth Colour Press, Parkstone, Poole.

Printed and bound in Singapore.

Contents

List of Illustrations

Introduction

The focus of this book is the Crucifixion of Christ from its earliest depiction in Christian art through to our own time. Each age has its own insights into the meaning of Christ's Passion, which is reflected in its art. I will be exploring that art and the Christian understanding which is reflected in it.

In order to give the book as sharp a focus as possible and keep it to a reasonable length I have not dealt at all with other pictures in the Passion cycle, such as the Arrest, the Betrayal by Judas with a kiss, the Flagellation, the Crowning with Thorns, the Carrying of the Cross, the Deposition, Lamentation and Entombment. Nor have I considered the Stations of the Cross, which developed from the fourteenth century onwards under Franciscan influence and which still today forms an important devotion in many churches. Each of the scenes in the Passion cycle has undergone its own development. But I have wanted to concentrate on the changes in a single image, that of Christ crucified. There is however one crucial exception.

The death of Christ cannot be considered apart from his Resurrection. For it is in the light of the Resurrection that the Cross is revealed as a victory. The Crucifixion of Jesus is not just one more example of human cruelty and tragedy. From a Christian standpoint it is God's victory over evil. But it was only in the light of the Resurrection that the first Christians were enabled to see this. The result is that in the earliest Christian art, as this book tries to show, the Cross and the Resurrection are seen in a unified manner as two aspects of one triumph. In particular I am concerned with the *Anastasis* (Greek for 'Resurrection'), the authorised image of the Orthodox Church for symbolically depicting Christ's victory over death. I have also used some pictures of the Resurrection appearances of Christ, when they first appear in the tradition or develop in a particular way. I have not tried to show how these have changed over the years (except in the case of the Anastasis) but have interspersed them with images of the Crucifixion as a constant reminder that Cross and Resurrection need to be seen together in art, as they are in theology. The book develops more or less chronologically with about one painting shown from each century. The exception is from the twentieth century when I have shown a few more. Even here of course I have been highly selective, and dozens more could have been shown if there had been space.

I am indebted to a number of important works of scholarship, which have been referred to in the footnotes. Those who wish to pursue the themes in this book should follow up those references. I am grateful to Professor Henry Mayr-Harting for personal help on the art of the Ottonian period.

+Richard Oxon
Oxford
September 2003

Figure 1a: Cross with P (for PAX) and alpha and omega in the Catacomb of Commodilla.

Figure 1b: Epitaph to Antonia, originally in the Catacomb of Domitilla. The cross as an anchor with two fishes.

Symbols in the Catacombs

— Second and Third Centuries —

Under the streets of present-day Rome, but outside the walls of ancient Rome, lie the Catacombs, many of which can be visited. These are not, as was once thought, places where Christians huddled in fear from persecution. They are burial places, which Christians used from the first to the fifth centuries. On the walls and at the end of the tombs are paintings and inscriptions, which give us a vivid insight into how Christians saw their faith, especially how they approached death.[1] Many of the scenes are taken from the Old Testament but nearly all of them, both Old Testament and New Testament scenes, express the hope of deliverance or salvation. Common pictures are Daniel in the lion's den, the three boys in the burning fiery furnace, the raising of Lazarus and the crossing of the Dead Sea. There are no surviving depictions of either the Crucifixion or the Resurrection of Christ and it seems that these Christians preferred to point to these foundation events through the wider theme of deliverance expressed in a number of different ways, but especially through the story of Jonah and the Whale.[2]

About 45,000 inscriptions survive from this ancient Christian period. More than half of them are in Rome and 75 per cent of these are of a funeral nature. About 13 per cent of these have an unambiguously Christian symbol, almost all centering on the word 'peace' in either Latin or Greek. These inscriptions begin to appear from the second and third centuries. The dead were buried in a series of horizontal shafts, stacked one above another, as if in bunk beds of stone. In order that the families could recognise their own departed, depictions of familiar goods associated with the deceased and inscriptions would be carved at the end of the shaft when it had been closed up. Shown here is a symbol from the catacomb of Commodilla.[3] The Cross is depicted but the vertical stroke also forms a P, which in this case is the first letter of the Latin word 'Pax', or Peace. On either side of the Cross of Peace are inscribed Alpha and Omega, the first and last letters of the Greek alphabet. As we read in Revelation 1:8

'I am the Alpha and the Omega' says the Lord God, who is and who was and who is to come, the Almighty.

The family of the person who had died put their trust in God, the beginning and the end of all things who through the Cross of his Son has brought us peace now and for eternity.

Those Christians, at first a tiny community subject from time to time to fierce persecution, must have had something of the feel of a secret society. So it is understandable that they should often prefer signs and symbols to a more overt visual expression of their faith. In the catacomb of Domitilla there is this epitaph of Antonia.[4] Today it can be seen in the Basilica of Sts Mereus and Achilleus. The anchor was already a symbol of hope in the Roman world but it took on a deeper meaning for Christians. The writer of the Epistle to the Hebrews, referring to the Christian hope of salvation through Christ, has these words: 'We have this as a sure and steadfast anchor of the soul' (Hebrews 6:19). This is no ordinary anchor however, for the crossbar has been transformed into a cross and, attached at either side to the hooks of the anchor, are two fishes. The fish was an important symbol in the early Church, first of all for Christ himself.

The letters of the Greek word for fish, ICTHUS, stand for 'Jesus Christ, Son of God, Saviour' (IESOUS CHRISTOS THEOU HUIOS SOTER), but because Jesus told his apostles to become 'fishers of men', Christians could also be referred to as 'fishes', swimming to salvation through the waters of baptism. The second-century theologian Tertullian wrote of baptism, 'But we small fishes, named after our great ICTHUS, Jesus Christ, are born in water and only by remaining in water can we live.' So here the family and friends of the loved one expressed their conviction that through our Christian faith we are fish being saved through the Cross of Christ, a sure anchor for our soul as we go through the waters of death.

Figure 2a: Sarcophagus with scenes from the Passion of Christ, Catacomb of Domitilla, mid-fourth century AD, Museo Pio Christiano, Vatican

The Victory of the Passion

— A Fourth-Century Sarcophagus —

This sarcophagus (stone carved coffin) found in the catacomb of Domitilla in Rome dates from the mid-fourth century.[5] The carvings on the side depict scenes from Christ's Passion, starting from the left as we look at it: Simon of Cyrene carrying the Cross with a soldier behind, then in the next panel Christ being crowned by a soldier. To the right of the central section the two scenes belong together. A large Christ stands in front of a soldier while both are looking towards Pilate in the next panel. But here Pilate looks away as two servants bring water and a bowl for him to wash his hands in.

Before looking at the central section in more detail it is important to note the theme of the wreath or crown which is so prominent.[6] A wreath hangs down from the pediment in both the left- and right-hand sections. Another one dominates the central panel, while just to the left Christ is being crowned, not so much with a crown of thorns as with a similar circlet of leaves: Christ, the emperor of God's new world.

Neither the word 'wreath' nor the word 'crown', both translations of the Greek word 'stephanos', convey the full meaning of these chaplets or circlets of leaves. For us a wreath is sometimes associated with mourning and sadness, but in the ancient world it was above all a sign of triumph. We think of crowns as being made of precious metal and jewels and associated only with royalty. But in antiquity crowns could be made of circlets of leaves and their use was very much wider than denoting monarchy; for example, winners of athletic or poetic contests were crowned with laurel wreaths. The gods were often depicted in this way, each god being associated with their own particular kind of leaf. No religious ceremony was complete without a wreath, either for the sacrificial animal, or the worshipper, or both. Such crowns were in fact primarily a religious rather than a royal symbol, for even games were dedicated to the gods. Above all, these crowns were used for the dead. As an ancient Roman writer put it: 'The crown is given to the dead as to those who have won in the contest of life.' Life was a contest and the deceased was the victor. So it was that wreaths or garlands (a form of extended wreath) came to be carved on the sides of Roman sarcophagi, indicating the triumph of a good life.

Christians were reluctant to take over the pagan custom of crowning their dead, for it is only Christ who can crown us. But they did not hesitate to use the metaphor of crowning: 'When the chief shepherd is manifested you will obtain the unfading crown of glory' (1 Peter 5:4) and 'Be faithful unto death, and I will give you the crown of life' (Revelation 2:10). So the four crowns carved in the side of this sarcophagus celebrate the victory of Christ's life, death and resurrection, in which Domitilla trusted. This is brought out by the selection and arrangement of the scenes. On the left a soldier strides behind Simon, who is carrying the Cross. But in the next panel it is a soldier who crowns Jesus. On the right-hand side, Pilate looks away defeated whilst hanging over him is the crown of Christ's victory, with Christ calm and confident in the next panel. All earthly power and rule gives way before him. This must have seemed particularly dramatic in the fourth century when the Emperor Constantine became a Christian and nearly three centuries of spasmodic persecution ended. All this is encapsulated in the central, dominating section which focuses on victory of Christ's death and resurrection. In the bottom half of the panel are depicted the two soldiers, one of whom is asleep, outside Christ's tomb, now empty for Christ has been raised.

So this is from one point of view the empty tomb, revealing that Christ has arisen. Yet it is not the risen Christ who is portrayed as in later Western art but the Cross. This Cross has a large wreath or crown in the upper half with, inside it, the first two letters in Greek of the word for Christ. The X(Chi)R(Ro) laid on top of one another to make what became in the fourth century the most pervasive of all Christian symbols. Here, depicted in symbolic form, is the resurrected, divine deliverer.

At the beginning of the fourth century there was, as so often, a civil war in the Roman Empire. Constantine, the Emperor in the West, prayed to God and saw a cross of light in the sky. Later, in a dream he was told to take a spear, put a bar across it and make a cross. Above this he was to put a wreath with a Chi-Ro sign in it as on this carving. Or at least this is the account of Eusebius, the first Church historian, who knew Constantine well. Constantine ordered his soldiers to adopt the Cross as a sign on their shields and won a decisive victory at the Battle of Milvian Bridge (in the year 312) which consolidated his position as ruler of the whole Empire. From this time on the imperial standard or 'labarum', had a Chi-Ro sign either surmounting or superimposed upon it. See the coin of the Emperor Jovian (363–4) illustrated here. The Chi-Ro became the most distinctive Christian symbol

**Figure 2b: Coin of
Emperor Jovian**

until the sixth century, hence its use on this sarcophagus.[7] For Constantine and his soldiers this symbol pointed to the rule of God over the events of the world. The Christian God was indeed in control: how else could a small, persecuted Jewish sect become so widespread, even to the extent of gaining the allegiance of the Emperor himself? But for Domitilla and her family the meaning was deeper than the successful story of Christianity. It was about the victory of the Cross; a victory that endures whether the Church is expanding or contracting. This is the ultimate victory over sin and death, leading to eternal life with God.

Here for the first time we have a Christian monogram surrounded by a laurel wreath forming the central symbol of the Passion and Resurrection, all combined with a Cross. This unfading wreath of victory is placed below an eagle. The outstretched wings can be seen, though not very easily. The eagle was a symbol of Jupiter in Roman art and an indication of Roman triumph.

Above the wings of the eagle in either corner can be seen small figures of the sun (sol) and the moon (luna). These symbols will be discussed later (see p. 43) but in Roman art they were generally symbols of the victory and glory of the Empire and are seen in that role on the Arch of Constantine in Rome. Here on Domitilla's sarcophagus they refer to Christ's cosmic sovereignty and his eternal reign. In the Roman Empire portraits of victors were sometimes placed above the arm of the standard. Here we have not a portrait of Christ but a monogram indicating the victory of the Cross.

What is so crucial about the central section of this carved sarcophagus is that the Cross and the Resurrection are regarded as inseparable. This symbol of the Chi-Ro is at once the Cross and the Resurrection. The Resurrection is not some happy ending tacked onto the end of Christ's life on earth. It reveals the true meaning of the Cross: a life lived in self-surrender, which lives in God forever. From this victory of Christ's death and resurrection, peace comes to us all. Looking up at the wreath are two small doves. As a dove brought the message of God's peace to the world after the flood in Genesis, so the Holy Spirit brings the message of Christ's peace: the peace that comes through reconciliation with God and one another. The doves also symbolise the souls of faithful Christians participating in the victory and eternal life of Christ.

Roman culture was above all a visual culture, one which had a capacity continually to reinvent itself. When Christianity became the official religion of the Roman world it first adopted and then gradually transformed many familiar Roman images in such a way that they became part of a Christian narrative, controlled by Christian belief. Greek myth gave way to the Christian story. The emperor, omnipresent through his image, remains but points to the supreme emperor, for whom he was viceregent on earth; through this visual display viewers were enabled to participate imaginatively in mystical, eternal realities.[8]

So Christians in the fourth century looking at a sarcophagus like this would have been made aware of a number of interconnected, mutually reinforcing themes. First, and most apparent, was the fact that the Roman empire was now a Christian empire. The soldiers who had once arrested Christ, brought him to Pilate and who walked behind Simon of Cyrene carrying the Cross were now soldiers in Christ's cause. Second, the lord of history, carrying all before him, was none other than Jesus Christ who had been raised from the dead. The first letters of his name, X P, appeared on the imperial banner, juxtaposed with the cross, within a wreath of victory. Third, the approach of Jesus to his death was to be seen not as that of a helpless victim, but a divine conqueror, as Bishop Venantius Fortunatus (503–609) was to emphasise in his famous sequence of passiontide hymns with its opening line 'The royal banners forward go'. Finally, the believer laid in this sarcophagus, or looking upon it, would have confidence that the same victory over death and all the powers of evil had, through faith and baptism, become theirs.

**Figure 3: Christ's Victory on the Cross, juxtaposed with the suicide of Judas,
AD 420–30, now in the British Museum**

The First Depiction of Christ
on the Cross

— A Fifth-Century Ivory —

One of the earliest surviving examples of Christ shown on the Cross is one of four small ivory panels, probably from a casket, which may have held relics, made in the Roman West about 420 AD. It juxtaposes the image of Christ alive and reigning from the Cross with that of Judas hanging dead from a tree. On another panel, three scenes from the Passion are compressed together: Christ carrying the Cross, Pilate washing his hands and Peter denying Christ. A third panel shows the two women finding the tomb of Christ empty and in a fourth the risen Christ appears to a doubting Thomas and the other disciples. The plaques are elegantly worked in high relief. Although the heads are unnaturally large, the figures are realistic with graceful draperies. There is one other depiction of Christ crucified from this period, about 432, carved in wood on the door of the Church of St Sabina in Rome, which seems crude by comparison with the ivory carving shown here. It is iconographically also very different. In the wooden carving, Christ is flanked by two thieves; all the figures are inexpressive and they appear against an architectural background in which the Cross is scarcely visible. When these four ivory panels, housed in the British Museum, are considered as a whole, their dominant iconographic message is that of a victorious, divine Christ. Pilate and Peter appear in the first panel because they were both troubled by a dawning recognition of who Christ was. In the next panel Christ strides confidently to his death, whilst in the following one he is depicted on the Cross as muscular, strong and fully alive. The third panel reveals that death cannot hold him and the fourth shows him, having overcome evil, showing himself to Thomas and confidently sending out the disciples to continue his victorious work.[9]

But why were the first Christians so reluctant to show Christ crucified on the Cross? This and the one on the St Sabina church door are both the earliest we have and the only ones known from the fifth century. Although we have a wonderful and comprehensive display of sixth-century mosaics in Ravenna, on several churches and baptisteries, not a single one depicts Christ on the Cross. One reason may be that the Crucifixion was, quite simply, a form of public execution, a horrible judicial torture. To an onlooker, crucifixion conveyed not only agony but disgrace. If in the days of public hanging a religious sect had adopted the gallows, with one of its members swinging on it, as their symbol, it would have struck eighteenth- and nineteenth-century society as a deliberate affront, an assertion of lawlessness. Christians in the early centuries were subject to spasmodic persecution. Moreover, we know that from as early as the New Testament, they wanted to present themselves as respectable and responsible citizens of the Roman world, identifying with the best elements within it. Those who knew Christians knew of course that the one they worshipped had been crucified, and Christians could be mocked for this. There is a graffiti of an ass being crucified, with the words, 'Anexagoras worships his God', which may very well be a mocking attack on a Christian slave. So there was little motive to display Christ on the Cross and every social reason why this should not be done, even though of course the Cross was a central element in Christian preaching of the period.

Nevertheless, at the end of the fourth century and during the fifth, Christians did begin to depict Christ on the Cross. This clearly had something to do with the fact that the Emperor Constantine abolished crucifixion as a form of public execution when he became a Christian some time after 312. Later, the Emperor Theodosius had all pagan temples and statues destroyed. It was fitting, then, for Christ to be shown on the Cross, for his death would no longer be interpreted as the death of a criminal but the saving act of a God in whom even the Emperor now believed.[10]

In later Christian history, particularly from the thirteenth century onwards, Christ's suffering on the Cross was greatly emphasised. It is important to realise however that the classical world may not have seen, and indeed did not see, suffering in the way that later Christians understood it. For example, in 1506, when the now famous Laocoön sculpture was first unearthed, the depiction of the Trojan priest and his two sons being strangled by a serpent was admired by people of the time as an example of heroic suffering by those who deserved pity. But this is not how the classical world perceived the sculpture. Heroism was shown stoically, by calm endurance. Laocoön's agony, for them, was a sign of his justified punishment: the Roman writer Epictetus described grief as a revolt against the divine order and 'Laocoön's protestations amount to the histrionics of impiety.'[11]

Although the late fourth century provided the historical conditions for

Christ to be shown on the Cross for the first time, there is a deeper reason why Christians were reluctant to do this earlier. It is because their faith was above all a faith in Christ's conquest of evil, a conquest inseparable from his Resurrection. As already mentioned, Christian frescoes in the Catacombs were all on the theme of deliverance and salvation. The fourth-century Passion sarcophagus discussed earlier makes the point even more powerfully. The first Christians wished to emphasise that Christ was risen, that is, he had overcome death and conquered evil. He would come again to judge the living and the dead. This was what mattered to them. Nevertheless, by about 400, Christ is shown on the Cross, as on this ivory plaque. But this is no defeated Christ: his eyes are open and head upright, and his arms stretch firmly outwards. He looks boldly to the front, not so much constrained by the Cross as superimposed upon it. The contrast is deliberately made with Judas hanging on the tree, the thirty pieces of silver spilled out onto the ground at his feet. The branch bends, almost breaking, with his weight. The other wood, the wood of the Cross, proudly displays REX IUD, King of the Jews. Judas is dead and defeated, but Christ is alive with the life of triumphant love. Around the Cross Mary and John to one side look forlorn, while on the other side, Longinus, according to legend the soldier who thrust the spear into Christ's side, looks angry or amazed. Over this anger and sadness and death the love of God wins through. Christ reigns from the tree.

Figure 4: The Marys at the Tomb. Ravenna, Church of Sant' Apollinare Nuovo

The Women Discover the Empty Tomb

— A Sixth-Century Mosaic —

The gospels are silent about the actual process of Christ's Resurrection. There is no account of what happened to his body during the days in the tomb or how he might have been raised. This reticence is carried over into early Christian art and was reinforced by doctrinal considerations: any attempt to show Christ's actual rising would have been in danger of getting the balance wrong between his divinity and his humanity, a subject of fierce controversy at the time. Christian artists got round this problem by witnessing to Christ's Resurrection through the women's discovery of the empty tomb.

According to Matthew's account (Matthew 28:1–10), Mary Magdalen and Mary (whom we know from Mark's gospel the mother of James) come to the tomb. They are confronted by an angel sitting upon the rolled-back stone, who says to them: 'Do not be afraid; for I know that you seek Jesus who was crucified. He is not here; for he has arisen, as he said. Come, see the place where he lay. Then go quickly and tell his disciples that he has risen from the dead, and behold, he is going before you to Galilee; there you will see him' (Matthew 28:5–7).

This scene is traditionally called 'the Myrophores', from the Greek word meaning 'perfume bearers', because according to Mark 16:1 the women were going to the tomb to anoint Christ's dead body. This therefore is the main way in which the Church witnessed to the Resurrection in art during the early centuries of Christianity.

On the eastern edge of the Roman Empire, on the borders of the Persian Empire, was the frontier town of Dura-Europos. It is here that we have the earliest surviving evidence of a Christian baptistery and house church, dating about 230. On the walls of the baptistery, there is a picture of women approaching a tomb, very much in the Roman manner. The same scene forms one of the panels on the ivory of about 420 in the British Museum already discussed. The large reproduction shown here comes from the Church of St Apollinare Nuovo in Ravenna. It is but one scene of an interesting narrative cycle on the upper walls. This wonderful basilica, dating from the first third of the sixth century, has the largest expanse of mosaics that have been preserved from the ancient world. The style is Byzantine, rather than late antique as in the ivory plaque considered in the previous section. The tomb depicted is no ordinary one but is a picture of the Rotunda built over the place where Christ was buried and from which he was raised, in Jerusalem. After Constantine became emperor, his mother Helena travelled to the Holy Land and located many of the places associated with the life of Jesus, in particular, the sites where he had been crucified and then buried. Constantine built a church over the site and, about the year 350, a rotunda within the church was erected over the tomb. This is the church, much rebuilt and altered, of the Holy Sepulchre which can be seen in Jerusalem today, a church which should properly be called the Church of the Anastasis or Resurrection, for it is this which is celebrated, not the burial.[12]

In this mosaic from the Church of St Apollinare Nuovo, the two women point towards the empty tomb. Although in some early depictions three women are shown (as in Mark's account), two women became the established norm. On the other side of the tomb entrance the angel points upwards, witnessing to Christ's rising. This scene witnessed to the Resurrection in two ways. First, the Rotunda would bring to mind the historical basis of the events in the life of Jesus. The actual site had been located and a church built upon it. A rotunda like this had been erected over the tomb. Secondly, the women had seen for themselves that the tomb was empty and had encountered an angel with the message that Christ had arisen.

In the depiction on the British Museum ivory, this message is reinforced by another detail. On the door of the tomb is a picture of Christ raising Lazarus. This image often appeared on the walls of the Catacombs and was one of the main ways in which the first Christians felt comfortable about expressing their belief in Christ risen. For Jesus had said to Martha, before he raised her brother Lazarus, 'I am the Resurrection and the Life; he who believes in me, though he die, yet shall he live, and whoever lives and believes in me shall never die' (John 11:25).

In the mosaic shown here the door of the tomb is shown in the Rotunda as a rhomboid. In some later depictions of this scheme, this rhomboid became in itself a sign of Christ's Resurrection.[13] A stone relief, now in the Dumbarton Oaks collection in Washington DC, for example, simply shows the Rotunda, with an empty square signifying the tomb, and a free-floating rhomboid, signifying the stone rolled away from the tomb. Below is an empty cross, so that the whole image, symbolic in a minimalistic way, indicates both the saving Passion and Christ's Resurrection.

After the eighth century, the tomb was often depicted as an empty cave, but during this early Byzantine period the image of the Rotunda in the Church of the Anastasis at Jerusalem was a reassuring reference for Christian believers.

Although our sceptical minds will continue to ask critical questions about why the tomb was empty, two undeniable facts still remain. First, there was never any attempt by the Christian community to form a cult around the grave of Jesus. The very natural human tendency, when a great figure dies, to erect a monument over the grave and develop a cult centred on it never happened with the body of Jesus. It was not until thirty years after his death that the place of his death and resurrection was made a focus and the emphasis then was on this as the place of the Resurrection. Second, no opponent of the first Christians ever produced his body. The whole Christian message could have been exploded as false by producing Jesus' dead body. This was never done. The story of the discovery of the empty tomb, and its depiction in art, confronts us as it confronted the first Christians, with the mystery of Christ: for Christian believers, the mystery of Christ risen.

So it was that when Christians made a pilgrimage to the Holy Land, sometimes they returned with the memento of a small flask (an ampulla) with a picture on it of the women discovering the tomb empty. Some of these have survived from the sixth century.[14]

Figure 5: The Crucifixion and Resurrection seen together. From the Rabbula Gospels

Christy in a Long Tunic

— A Sixth-Century Gospel Book —

Evidence of how Christians saw the Christian faith in its first centuries is gained from frescoes on the walls of the catacombs, sarcophagi, ivories and mosaics. These four different kinds of material were used in the depictions so far discussed. Another invaluable source of evidence is provided by the illustrations from illuminated manuscripts. The scene depicted here comes from the Rabbula Gospels which were completed in the year 586. The calligrapher Rabbula was probably the head of the Scriptorium (the room in the monastery where manuscripts were written and illustrated) in the Monastery of St John in Zagby, north of Apameia in present-day Syria. By the sixth century AD, Eastern and Western forms of Christianity had begun to develop distinguishing features. Constantine had founded Constantinople in 330 as a new, Christian, Rome, ostensibly the capital of the whole empire. Rome retained much of its prestige, particularly with the old, sometimes still pagan, families, but had been devastated by invasions, particularly its capture in 410. The text of the Rabbula Gospels manuscript is in Syriac, therefore written for use in a Syriac-speaking community, though the artist may have had access to Byzantine manuscripts with New Testament illustrations.

This depiction of the Passion is important and interesting from a number of different points of view. Christ is shown in a colobium, a long sleeveless tunic, more substantial than the normal chiton or tunic. This contrasts with how Christ is shown in the British Museum ivory discussed earlier where he is naked except for a loincloth. Christ here is shown with a beard, a tradition which became definitive in the East, whereas before he was shown beardless. He is also nailed through the ankles rather than the feet. He is alive on the Cross, with no signs of failing. The question of why Christ was shown alive or dead on the Cross will be considered later (see p. 29).

But this depiction by Rabbula can helpfully be compared with a wall painting in the Theodotus Chapel of the Church of St Maria Antiqua in Rome, dated 741–52, in which Christ is also shown in a colobium and very much alive. In contrast to this and the description here is an icon at Sinai which may date from the eighth century, in which Christ is again shown wearing a colobium, but he appears with eyes closed and a crown of thorns on his head, indicating his suffering and death.[15]

What is perhaps of most significance about the Rabbula version of the Passion is the fact that immediately below the Cross and aligned with it is the empty tomb. The tomb is wide open, with the guards as it were thrust back by the force of an explosion. Although at this stage Christian artists were still very reluctant to probe the mystery of Christ's Resurrection, they were clearly interested in what really happened during the three days in the tomb. Indeed, Christian preachers of the time were not content to think of him simply lying dead in the grave. Christ could not possibly be kept under the bonds of death but rose instead as the sun/Son of Righteousness in the underworld, where his soul flashed forth the light of its divinity and destroyed the Kingdom of Hades. At this stage they did not depict the conquest of Hades in art but they did indicate the effect of this explosion of light on the tomb and the guards. The Resurrection is understood and visualised here as a veritable explosion of light bursting open the door of the tomb, overthrowing its three guards in the process.

It is highly significant that this scene is just below and aligned with the Cross. Before this date the Resurrection was mainly depicted by showing the two women talking to an angel at the empty tomb, as in the mosaic in St Apollinare Nuovo, already discussed, or approaching the empty tomb as in the fifth-century Roman plaque referred to earlier. But here the women and the angel have been put to one side, whilst on the other the risen Christ is shown greeting them, in the scene known as 'the Chairete', from the Greek word meaning 'greeting'. So the lower register is dominated by the empty tomb, with the door flung open and the guards falling about. What the illustrator wishes to convey is the integral unity of the Cross and Christ risen. In the upper register the soldiers thrust a spear and sponge at him: but in the lower one, as it were, counterbalancing this and revealing its true meaning, Christ is shown as triumphant over the forces of evil. In the words of the old Easter carol, Christ has burst his three-day prison. Above is Christ apparently in the power of men: below, that powerlessness is revealed to be the power of God which is stronger than men. Above, life is about to be extinguished; below, his life is shown as indestructible. For this is the life of God which can only be revealed not taken away. The artist does not want to show the dead body of Christ on the Cross or that dead body being taken down and entombed. He does not wish even to concentrate on the women finding the tomb empty. His focus is on the unified vision of Christ at once crucified and risen.

Figure 6a: North Cross, Ahenny, Co. Tipperary, East Face

On the Edges of Empire

— Signs in Stone from the Seventh Century —

As discussed in an earlier section the Emperor Constantine, before the decisive battle in which he gained control of the Roman Empire as a whole, had a vision of a cross in the sky. He saw the words 'By this conquer'. The vision was followed by a dream of the Cross and in due course his soldiers adopted the Chi-Ro sign in a wreath of victory on their standards. Constantine's vision and his dream of the Cross were to be highly influential in early Christian literature and subsequent art.

During the fourth century, the news quickly spread that Helena, Constantine's mother, had discovered the site of Jesus' crucifixion and had dug up pieces of his Cross. Pilgrims started to come to Jerusalem to venerate the wood of the 'the true Cross'. There they venerated a large wooden cross, covered in precious metal and jewels, that had been erected on Golgotha. That image came to be a most powerful one which was carried and reproduced to the ends of the Roman world and beyond.

In the Church of St Pudenziana in Rome, there is an apse mosaic from the fourth century depicting this *Crux Gemmata* (Jewelled Cross) standing on the hill of Golgotha. But it was at the edges of the Empire, rather than in Rome itself, that the influence of this Cross was to be most persistent: to the East in Georgia and Armenia, and outside the Empire to the West, in Ireland. In these distant parts, that is, distant from the centres of late antique and Byzantine civilisation, it was not in mosaic, ivory, or wood that this image of the Cross appeared and survived, but in stone.

The finding of the Cross by Helena was celebrated annually in a Church feast. But this became overlaid and superseded by a further variation on the Cross. Jerusalem had been captured by the Persians but, in 629, the Emperor Heraclius recaptured it. Triumphantly he returned the Cross to its proper place and held it up to be honoured. So the feast became one of the uplifting or exaltation of the Cross. In art, the themes of Constantine's vision and dream, Helena's finding of the Cross, together with the associated stories and the uplifting by Heraclius, became intertwined and brought to the West by the Crusaders. For example, there is a fascinating 'Wheel Cross' at Kello in County Durham dating from about 1200 which has the carvings associated with these scenes on the pillar supporting the Cross. In the fifteenth century Piero della Francesca painted this cycle in the Church of St Francis in Arezzo and there are well-preserved examples from the sixteenth century in churches in Cyprus.[16] That development is a fascinating story but our concern here are the stone crosses which appeared in Ireland, Wales and parts of Scotland from the fifth century, particularly from the seventh to the ninth centuries.[17] These crosses show the influence of pre-Christian menhirs (standing stones) and carry Celtic decorative motifs. See the seventh-century pillar stone at Reask, County Kerry, illustrated below where the incised cross has been adapted to local artistic traditions. See also the ninth/tenth-century Muiredach's cross at Monasterboice also illustrated here. But their most interesting feature is their continuity with the large jewelled cross that pilgrims from the fourth century onward saw erected in Jerusalem.

**Figure 6b: Seventh-
century Pillar Stone at
Reask, Co. Kerry**

Figure 6c: Ninth/tenth-century Muiredach's Cross

In the parish church of Ruthwell, not far from Dumfries in south-west Scotland, there is a stone cross more than five metres high. Part of the text of a poem known as 'The Dream of the Rood' or 'The Vision of the Cross' is carved on the stone in Runic symbols. This remarkable, moving poem tells the story of the Crucifixion from the standpoint of the wood of the Cross, which shares in the suffering of Christ. In a dream the poet sees:

> The tree itself
> Borne on the air, light wound about it,
> – A beam of brightest wood, a beacon clad
> In overlapping gold, glancing gems
> Fair at its foot, and five stones
> Set in a crux flashed from the Cross tree.
>
> Around angels of God
> All gazed upon it,

> Since first fashioning fair.
> It was not a felon's gallows,
> For Holy Ghosts beheld it there,
> And men on mould, and the whole making shone for it
> – *Signum* of victory!

This was no bare cross, still less a decoration. It was a *signum*, a sign of victory. And it was the Cross set up at Golgotha in Jerusalem, wood covered in gold and jewels, that the poet has in mind.

This can be seen clearly in the Cross illustrated on p. 22, the North Cross at Ahenny in County Tipperary.[18] This cross of stone seeks to give the impression of being a wooden cross covered in plates of gold or gilded metal and studded with jewels. For example, the bosses are in high relief with hatched moulding. Two other details are highly significant. First, the cross has a cap on the top, which is a visual reflection of the canopy that Constantine placed over the Holy Sepulchre in Jerusalem. Second, the cross here is on a stepped base. The representation in the apse at St Pudenziana shows the Cross on Golgotha and where it was not possible to show Golgotha as such, steps were shown to represent it. This is so not only for the crosses in the West but also those in Armenia and Georgia, which have their own distinctive style. See for instance the example from Armenia illustrated here. Those from Armenia often show foliage – representing new life – growing from under and out from the Cross.[19] But there are certain key similarities. The setting-up of stone crosses was a key element in the conversion of Georgia, Armenia and Ireland. No doubt such crosses were set up elsewhere as well, but these are not available to us. Some from the edges of the Empire are. Through wind and weather, wars and devastation of many kinds, those stone crosses have survived, a sign of Christ's victory.

**Figure 6d:
Example of an
Armenian Cross**

Figure 7: Christ Dead on the Cross. Mosaic from Hosios Loukas

Christ Dead on the Cross

— An Eleventh-Century Mosaic —

In the earliest depictions of the Passion that have survived, Christ is shown alive on the Cross. This was true both in the West (for example, the British Museum ivory and the door of the Church of St Sabina, in Rome) and the East (the Rabbula Gospels). The reason for this and the eventual move to show Christ dead on the Cross is intimately related to the theological controversies of the time. In those days theology was a matter of crucial, popular debate that is difficult to imagine now. People from all backgrounds argued vigorously about the latest theological disputes in the streets. Given the sensitivity of these subjects, artists did not feel free to depict Christ just in any way that happened to please them. In showing Christ they could not avoid making a doctrinal point.

The major theological issue that concerned the Church from the fourth to the eighth centuries, in one aspect or another, was the person of Christ. The Church came to assert that he is truly God and truly human, yet he remains one undivided person. If this is the case then how should Christ be depicted on the Cross? If he was simply shown dead, or in the tomb, people might wonder what had happened to his divinity. So it would seem that from the fourth to the end of the seventh centuries artists chose to avoid these controversial questions by not showing him dead on the Cross at all. Christ is shown, as we have seen, with arms outstretched, head upright and eyes open, very much alive. This had the doctrinal advantage of making it clear that Jesus had indeed been crucified as a human being, for there he was on the Cross. But his open eyes could be interpreted as the *logos*, the eternal word of God described in John 1:1–14, the divine word being very much awake.

This began to change at the end of the seventh century and during the first half of the eighth century when Christ was first shown dead on the Cross. It seems that the Church had resolved its doctrinal dilemmas, leaving the way open to find artistic ways to represent all aspects of the truth. Christ would be shown dead on the Cross, indicating he was indeed fully human, going through a death like ours. At the same time his human soul would be shown united to the divine *logos* in Hades, the abode of the dead, overcoming death in the depiction known as the Anastasis. The point here is that at this time the Church finally had enough confidence in its doctrinal formulations to show Christ truly dead on the Cross.

The theological rationale of this was worked out in a work known as the *Hodegos* by Anastasius Sinaites towards the end of the seventh century,[20] and it is in the first half of the eighth century that we have the earliest surviving example of a dead Christ on the Cross on a portable icon in the monastery of St Catherine on Mount Sinai. There the dead Christ on the Cross is balanced by symbols of his divinity, the wearing of the colobium, the presence of angels and the sun and moon.

In the British Museum ivory discussed earlier, Christ is shown dressed only in a loin-cloth. In the Rabbula Gospels he is fully covered in a colobium. In the East, both modes of dress continue to appear, whether Christ is depicted alive or dead. In the West, the depiction of Christ naked on the Cross except for a loin-cloth, as in the British Museum, was found somewhat shocking but was allowed provided he was shown fully alive. It was therefore something of a shock for Western observers coming to the East in the eleventh century to discover that Christ was not only depicted in a loin-cloth but was shown dead on the Cross. Cardinal Humbert in 1054, in his anathema of the Eastern Church, stated amongst other charges the question 'How do you come to fasten to Christ's Cross the picture of a dying man?' In fact, as will be seen in subsequent sections, the West *had* started to depict Christ dead on the Cross, dressed only in a loin-cloth but this was only in northern Europe. Cardinal Humbert was shocked by what he saw because he was familiar with the art of Italy, where this was not yet depicted.

The mosaic shown here comes from the lovely monastery of Hosios Loukas, in Greece just to the north of the Gulf of Corinth. It dates from 1022 when orthodox iconography had become standardised after the theological disputes of previous centuries. It is a depiction like this which would have shocked Cardinal Humbert and his colleagues. For Christ is shown dead, eyes closed and head on one side, wearing only a loin-cloth and with blood pouring from his hands and side and feet and the body sagging sideways. Like other scenes from the gospels in Hosios Loukas, it is depicted with a monumental simplicity: 'There is no suggestion of historical narrative; the scene is a reminder of a historical feast.'[21]

In this standard portrayal only Mary the mother of Christ and John the beloved disciple are shown, Mary with hand pointing to Jesus and John with his head on his hand. Above them are some of the words in Greek from John

19:26 and 27: 'When Jesus saw his mother and the disciple whom he loved standing near, he said to his mother, "Woman, behold your son!" Then he said to the disciple, "Behold your mother!" And from that hour the disciple took her to his own home.'

Above the Cross is the Greek word for the Crucifixion and above that the sun and moon, shown as discs with faces inside. Over them are the initial letters in Greek of the words Jesus Christ. Below the Cross, the hill of Golgotha is shown with the skull of death, upon which blood from the body of Christ is flowing.

The changes in the way Jesus is depicted on the Cross in the Byzantine world can be traced in a number of different media besides mosaic, such as ivory, wall paintings and enamel. For example, the State Museum of Fine Arts in Georgia holds cloisonné enamels from both the eighth and tenth centuries showing Christ upright and alive on the Cross. There is a similar eighth-century enamel from Constantinople in the Metropolitan Museum of Art in New York, while the Georgian museum also has a tenth-century enamel depicting Jesus clearly dead, blood flowing from his side into a chalice.[22]

Through the centuries of theological discussion the Church clearly grasped the point that if the divine logos had become truly human, this meant undergoing a human death, the kind of death we all must experience. So the mosaicist of Hosias Loukas has the faith, the faith of the Church, to depict Christ truly dead on the Cross. As the early Christian hymn puts it, Christ 'Humbled himself and became obedient unto death, even on a Cross' (Philippians 2). For love of us God was prepared to undergo the obliteration of death. Yet in faith, the Church believes that his death has overcome death. Legend had it that Adam, the first man, a symbol of humanity as a whole, was buried in Golgotha. In this mosaic, the redeeming blood of Christ, the true man who redeems humanity, pours onto the skull of Adam. So although Christ's death is shown, this is also a death that brings humanity hope.

Figure 8: *The Incredulity of Thomas.* Monastery of Hosios Loukas

Doubting Thomas

— A Byzantine Mosaic —

We have seen the first depiction of Christ on the Cross, an ivory plaque
dating from about 420 and now in the British Museum. That scene was one
of a set of four, another being the appearance of the risen Christ to Thomas.
Thomas is shown pointing at a wound in Christ's left side. Christ holds his
left hand high and three other disciples are present. This scene, known in the
East as the 'Incredulity of Thomas', depicts an important witness to the
Resurrection of Christ from an early stage. It did not however replace the
Myrophores, that is, the scene of the women finding the tomb empty, but
was used to reinforce the message of the Resurrection. For example,
ampullae from the sixth and seventh centuries have been found with
Myrophores painted on one side and the Incredulity of Thomas on the other.
By the tenth century, this scene had become part of the standard cycle of
gospel pictures, as in this mosaic from Hosios Loukas (1022). In the same
church, in the crypt, there is a wall painting of this scene which is slightly
later: 'The consistent difference between the mosaics and the wall paintings
is the increase in narrative effects in the crypt, contrasting with the clear and
direct images in mosaic.'[23] There is also a similar mosaic at Daphni dating
from around 1100. In the mosaic shown here Thomas (whose face has been
erased) holds up his hand to touch the wound in Christ's right side as Christ
himself holds up his right hand. On either side of the pair are five apostles,
Judas being absent. Heading the group on the right is Peter, known by his
white curly hair and beard. On the left, the group is led by Paul with his bald,
domed forehead. Paul's high forehead, pronounced eyebrows, long nose and
penetrating gaze are intended to convey his intellectual pre-eminence
through an imposing physical presence. The tradition of depicting Paul and
Peter in this manner was fixed as early as the fourth century. However the
Acts of Paul and Thecla on which the traditional description is partly based
also describes Paul as being short and bandy-legged! The Acts is an
apocryphal work, dating from the second century, which was very popular
in the early Church.[24]

According to the Gospels, of course, Paul's encounter with the risen Christ did not come until later, but in early Christian and Byzantine art he is shown present at the Ascension, the Pentecost and here in the room with other apostles before the risen Christ.

Christ is an impressive figure, appearing against a background of a door, which became a standard part of the iconography of this scene. Above the door in Greek are the words '*Ton Thuron Kekleismenon*', 'The doors were locked' (John 20:26). The ability of the risen Christ to appear whether doors or locked or not emphasises the miraculous nature of his risen presence. Of all the different aspects of the story which could have been selected for emphasis, it is on this that the scene was focused at that time. There is a profound insight here. Wherever we are, in a monastic cell or prison cell, whether the doors are open or closed, even if our circumstances or surroundings are constricting us, Christ can make himself known.

Figure 9: Anastasis from Daphni

The Anastasis

— An Eleventh-Century Mosaic —

The definitive way in which the Orthodox Church depicts the Resurrection of Christ is the scene known in the West as the Harrowing of Hell, or the Descent to Hell, and in the East simply as the Anastasis, the Greek word for resurrection. The example shown here, a mosaic in the church at Daphni near Athens dating from about 1100, shows all the main details of the scene as it had evolved over the previous four centuries. Christ stabs Hades/Satan with his great cross, the broken gates and bars of Hell lying around. With one hand Christ pulls Adam out of the grave, while next to him Eve pleadingly waits her turn. Next to her are King David and King Solomon. On the other side John the Baptist stands with raised arm indicating Christ. How did this vivid, powerful image originate and evolve?

First, there is a hint in the New Testament. In the First Letter to Peter it is written of Christ that he was 'put to death in the flesh but made alive in the spirit; in which he went and preached to the spirits in prison, who formerly did not obey, when God's patience waited in the days of Noah' (1 Peter 3: 18–20). This indicates that those who died before Christ had a chance to experience the risen Christ and hear the Gospel.

Second, there is a remarkable account of this descent into hell in the apocryphal work The Gospel of Nicodemus,[25] now dated not earlier than about 600 AD. This exists in various languages, including Greek and two early Latin versions, all slightly varying in detail, but the main outline remains clear. Because the Jewish authorities doubted the Resurrection of Christ, Joseph of Arimathea summoned up two witnesses, the sons of Simeon, who were amongst those whom Christ raised from the dead when he descended into the abode of the dead. These report how a great light broke into their darkness, and Psalm 24 was shouted exultantly:

> Lift up your heads, O ye gates, and be ye lift up, ye everlasting doors:
> And the King of Glory shall come in.
> Who is the King of Glory? It is the Lord strong and mighty, even the

Lord mighty in battle.
Lift up ye heads, O ye gates, and be ye lift up, ye everlasting doors:
And the King of Glory shall come in.
Who is the King of Glory: even the Lord of Hosts, he is the King of Glory.

The gates of hell are smashed and Satan bound. Christ lifts Adam from death with his right hand and the righteous dead depart into eternal life with him.

It is now thought that this account was not the main influence behind the early formation of the Anastasis image.[26] Nevertheless, it reveals the way Christians were thinking from the seventh century onward, and probably a great deal earlier; later images of the Anastasis took on some of the details of this story.

A third influence, and this time a visual one, behind the iconography of the scene was probably the way emperors were depicted liberating cities from their enemies. Roman coins over a number of centuries show the emperor with right hand outstretched and pulling a figure towards him, the figure a personification of the city being liberated. It would have been very natural for Christians to depict Christ the great liberator pulling Adam, that is, humanity, away from the clutches of death.[27]

Although the theme of Christ's descent to the abode of the dead and conquest of death had long been a theme of Christian preaching, it was only in the seventh century that conditions were conducive to this being expressed pictorially. As was suggested previously in the section on the eleventh-century mosaic at Hosios Loukas, it was during the seventh century that the Church finally resolved some of the difficult questions about the relationship between the divinity and humanity of Christ. Once resolved, artists felt able to show Christ dead on the Cross and then being buried. This was the death of his human body. But simultaneously with that death, Christ's soul, united to the eternal logos, descended to the abode of the dead and overcame the forces of evil, personified by Hades and Satan.

The first depiction of this was probably in the East, though the earliest surviving example dates from the seventh century in Rome. This is the Eastern-influenced fresco in the Church of St Maria Antiqua, which depicts Christ grasping Adam's wrist with his right hand and pulling him clear of the clutches of Hades. In succeeding centuries, the emphasis varies slightly and new themes come into prominence. Sometimes the stress is on the conquest of death, when Hades is shown spread-eagled and defeated, the broken bars, chains and keys of Hell lying about. Then later, as it were, to counterbalance this emphasis on the power of Christ's divinity, his real humanity is underlined. This is signified by the presence of the two kings, David (with a beard) and his son Solomon, appearing together. When they are depicted on their own, they have rather different meanings but here, together, they serve to emphasise that Christ was descended from Solomon and David in a human line. This message is reinforced by the early interpretations of Psalm 71 both by the theologian Origen in the first half of the third century and in pictorial form in a Gospel miniature in the seventh century.

Sometimes the emphasis shifts slightly away from the raising of Adam to Christ himself, the Resurrection and the Life. In the Hosias Loukas mosaic from about 1022, the focus is on him, bestriding the picture and sometimes facing to the front. Sometimes the emphasis is upon the saving work of Christ: the mosaic from Nea Moni on the island of Chios depicts Christ moving away from Adam, pulling him, and later Eve, clear of the grave with his right hand, while holding the Cross with his left. Then, again, in order as it were to get the balance right between the Passion and the Resurrection of Christ, in the Daphni mosaic illustrated here, the large patriarchal cross is shown stabbing down into the defeated Hades. Christ who dominates the mosaic pulls Adam from the grave with his left hand, while Eve pleads and David and Solomon stand behind. Opposite them John the Baptist, who prophesised that light would shine in our darkness, points to Christ, whilst behind him others await their turn.

The Anastasis is perhaps the most wonderful image devised by the Christian Church. Avoiding all literalism, it symbolises Christ's conquest over evil and death, holding out hope to the whole of humanity, the departed as well as the living. In the West, although this scene appears in a number of stone reliefs (and from about 1400 it is often depicted), its most powerful expression is in poetry and drama. Some of the most arresting of the mediaeval miracle plays re-enact the Anastasis. In the East, this icon quite naturally became mainly associated with Easter and the liturgy of Holy Saturday. Matins on Holy Saturday contains these words:

When you, life immortal,
Went down to death
You slew Hell
By your bright divine light.
When you raised the dead
From the deep sea earth,
The heavenly power shouted:
'Christ our God,
Giver of life,
Glory to you!'

Vespers on Holy Saturday contains these words:

> By your Passion, O Christ, we have been freed from passion;
> And by your Resurrection
> We have been ransomed from decay. Glory to you, Lord!
> Today Hell groans and cries out:
> My power has been destroyed.
> I received a mortal man
> As one of the dead.
> But I am completely unable to keep him prisoner,
> And with him I shall lose all my subjects.
> I held in my power
> The dead of all the ages.
> But look, he is raising them all.
> Glory to your Cross, Lord,
> And to your Resurrection!

**Figure 10: Ivory Crucifixion Plaque from Metz,
ninth century**

Classical and Cosmic

— A Carolingian Bookcover of the Crucifixion from the Ninth Century —

On Christmas Day, in the year 800, Charlemagne, the King of the Franks, was crowned Roman Emperor by the Pope. It marked an attempt to revise and re-establish the Roman Empire in the West and has given its name to a particular period of art, Carolingian, dating from Charlemagne's accession to the throne of the Franks in 768 until about the year 900.

The art of this period was a conscious attempt at *Renovatio*, the re-creation of the classical culture of the old Roman Empire. But it was not the pagan Empire that Charlemagne and his immediate successors valued, but the Christian Roman Empire of Constantine and Theodosius which they sought to re-establish.

Classical culture was not however the only influence on the art of this period. The anti-naturalistic linearism of the Celto-Germanic and Anglo-Saxon traditions also pervaded an art that survives in book illuminations, ivories and goldsmith work.

Under Constantine and Theodosius, the symbols and figures associated with Roman antiquity such as victories, tritons, nereids and so on had disappeared. But in the art of the Carolingian period these images were allowed to return and be set within a Christian context. For the first time they were tolerated in scenes of the Passion, as can be seen in the ivory panel illustrated here, which depicts the Crucifixion and was meant to be a bookcover. This panel was made in Metz in Germany during the third quarter of the ninth century and is now in the Victoria and Albert Museum in London.[28]

At the top in the centre in two circular plaques, set one above another, are the sun and moon personified. These figures had appeared in earlier depictions of the Crucifixion, for example, in the sixth-century illumination in the Rabbula Gospels, already discussed. They pick up a number of references to the sun and moon in the Bible, the creation of the greater and lesser light recorded in Creation (Genesis 1:16), in Joseph's dream, where the sun and moon and eleven stars bow down to him (Genesis 37:9), where the sun and moon praise God (Psalm 148:3), where the sun and moon are darkened (Joel 2:10), and where the sun and moon stand still (Habakkuk 3:11). These last two references are probably reflected in Mark 13:24 and its parallels in the other Gospels, when the sky is darkened at the Crucifixion. In the sixth and seventh centuries, there was some speculation about the sun and moon symbolising the divine and human nature of Christ. But here, the reference is probably a fairly straightforward one, namely the sun and moon as key aspects of creation looking down to Christ in sorrow, wonder and adoration.

On either side of the sun and the moon, two angels bend down to receive the soul of Christ, whilst in the second register, below the arms of the Cross Ecclesia, the figure of the Church receives blood from the side of Christ, symbolising the Eucharist, whilst on the other side the Synagogue, with a banner, looks up in awe. At either side of these are the familiar figures of Mary and John. By the Cross stand Longinus, with his lance, and Stephaton, with the sponge, people who appear in the apocryphal accounts of the Crucifixion. At the bottom of the second register, the dead emerge from circular mausolea. A snake winds around the upright at the foot of the Cross, symbolising Christ's cosmic conquest of evil, while below the snake in the bottom register, there are symbolic figures of Water, riding a sea monster and Earth, clutching her children to herself, and greenery coming from one hand.

By our tastes probably too much symbolism is crammed into this one small ivory but for people of the time it celebrated the truth of Christ's victory in as varied and rich a way as they knew how, drawing on a range of symbolism, classical and Christian. A similar approach can be seen in other crucifixes of the time, for example, a crucifix in the Museum of Cluny, Paris, where a snake is winding round the crucifix in an even more dramatic way.

The crucifix shown here is dotted with holes, which originally contained gold studs. It is in the characteristic style of the workshop of Metz, whose thick-set figures, with square jaws and straight noses, were swathed in heavy rounded loops of drapery.

What above all the artist wanted to convey and celebrate here was the universal, cosmic centrality of Christ crucified. The whole of creation is represented, and every aspect looks towards the figure on the Cross. In the top register angels, sun and moon look down. In the middle register, Church and Synagogue, the living and the dead look towards him, whilst below the feet the head of evil is trampled down. In the bottom register Earth with her children and Water look up – even the monster from the deep has his head raised. All things, visible and invisible, in heaven and on earth, the living and the departed, all look to Christ and gaze upon him.

Figure 11a: Crucifix commissioned by Archbishop Gero about 975 for Cologne Cathedral

A Sense of the Poignant

— An Ottonian Crucifix of the Tenth Century —

As mentioned earlier, when Cardinal Humbert went to Constantinople in 1054, he said he was shocked to see Christ portrayed dead on the Cross. This is surprising, for Christ had been shown this way in the West for some time. We must therefore assume that this was not the case in Italy, where Humbert lived, and that he had not visited the main centres of Christian art in what is now Germany. For it was in these places that there was less inhibition about showing the dead Christ, as any other dead human being.

The Ottonian dynasty (919–1024 or later), originating in what is now Germany, reversed the disintegration of the Carolingian empire and

Figure 11b: Close-up of Gero Crucifix

consolidated an empire which included parts of France and Italy. Like the
Carolingians, the Ottonian Kings saw themselves as heirs of the old
Christian Roman world, while at the same time retaining their own native,
Saxon traditions. Ottonian rulers were even more concerned than the
Carolingians to show Christ as king, in a way which reinforced the sacral
basis of their own royal rule. For example, the Uta Codex, produced in
Regensburg about 1020, emphasised the cosmic rule of Christ from the
Cross more vividly than almost any other depiction in any period. At the
same time, artists at this time were not afraid to show the human death of
Jesus in all its starkness. Bishop Abraham of Freising (957–94)
commissioned a sacramentary in which Christ is shown with eyes closed
and head falling forwards. Although he is in a long robe, it is not a purple
robe which would indicate royal rule. Instead of being larger than life size,
towering over the figures of Mary and John, he is the same size, almost
embracing them with his outstretched arms.

What above all is significant about this picture is what is left out. Contrast
the Freising sacramentary with the Sinai icon, mentioned earlier, which was
the first depiction of Christ dead on the Cross from the East that has been
preserved, and still retains symbols of his kingly status: angels descend from
heaven to receive him, and the sun and moon, symbols of his eternal
authority, are present.

During the time of Bishop Abraham there was a debate about the
relationship between the divinity and the humanity of Christ and how they
should be depicted. A priest, Rihkar, wrote a letter to Abraham concerning
Christ:

> From his assumption of humanity, he was affected by fasts, overcome with sleep,
> oppressed by insults and jeers, bound, taken captive, scourged, cuffed round his
> ears, held in derision, crucified at the end, pierced with a lance, kept down for a
> space by death, buried, and then on the third day, having conquered death, he was
> raised again. This we confess by our catholic faith.[29]

Rihkar asked Bishop Abraham to judge between this view and those who
opposed it. It seems clear from the crucifixion which Abraham
commissioned that he sympathised with this stress on Christ's humanity.
Similarly, amongst the crucifixes associated with Bernward of Hildeshein
(993–1022), there is one that shows Christ dead and slumped forward on the
Cross. It is against the background of this development that we must view
the greatest of the crucifixes of this period, one commissioned by
Archbishop Gero of Cologne about 975 and illustrated here. Its

commissioning in Cologne, where it is still present in Cologne Cathedral, is of itself significant. For amongst the various artistic schools in the Ottonian Empire, it was above all in Cologne that the humanity of Christ was stressed.

In the Gero Crucifix there is no concentration on suffering as such. Rather, what is caught and conveyed is the sheer weight of Christ's body, hanging, yet in repose. The head falls forward, the arms are pulled down, the skin is stretched across the chest and the body bends to the right, whilst the legs move back to the Superdaneum (the wooden rest for the feet) in graceful parallel. The body is helpless, passive. Yet at the same time there is dignity and serenity, conveyed in the fine, graceful lines. There is restraint here, the kind of restraint that at once hides and conveys powerful emotion. For it is poignant without any suggestion of emotional bludgeoning. The suffering is accepted rather than abject.

There is a remarkable story in the *Chronicle of Thietmar of Merseburg* about Gero and this crucifix. The wooden head of Christ was seen to be split, so Gero placed a Host from the Eucharist and a relic of the Cross in the crack. He then 'Prostrated himself, and in tears called on the name of the Lord'. The Host is described as 'His one solace amongst troubles'.[30] Perhaps it was the crack in the crucifix which suddenly made his troubles unbearable and brought forth his tears, tears for both the troubles of his time, and the suffering of the Saviour. Perhaps also it was for the gift of tears that he had been praying, like some of his contemporaries. Whatever the reason, deep feeling is involved, feeling which is depicted with great artistic delicacy and genius in the crucifix.

For understandable reasons, both theological and political, the Ottonian rulers emphasised the majesty of Christ. More surprisingly, they also wanted to incorporate his humility into their political ideology. The theme of the life of Mathilda, the mother of Otto I, is dignity with humility (*dignitas cum humilitati*). Of course Christians have always emphasised humility. But what appears to have been distinctive about the Ottonian rulers was first the idea that humility could be a way to glory, taking up a theme in St Luke's Gospel, and second that the ideal of humility and humiliation could be associated with royalty in an integral way.

This political ideology is seen at its most vivid and dramatic in the Lothair Cross in Aachen Cathedral, dated from about the year 1000. On one side, the side that faced the people as it was carried in procession down the Cathedral aisle, is a finely worked golden cross studied with jewels. In the centre is a fine cameo of the Emperor Augustus, crowned with a wreath. On the other side of the cross however, the side that faced the Emperor as he walked in procession down the aisle, is a relief of Christ crucified. Christ is shown with his head falling down to his right side and his body twisted out to the left; he is clearly dead, with blood flowing from his hands and side and feet, and without any Eucharistic symbolism. But above the figure a hand descends from heaven holding a wreath to be placed on Christ's head, with a dove within the wreath. While the people saw the glory of the cross, the Emperor was face to face with Christ's divine suffering. It seems that religious devotion to the suffering of Jesus at Gorze, Freising and at Cologne was so powerful that it was incorporated in the political ideology of the royal family. Furthermore, already in the tenth century relics of the Passion were venerated in the monasteries and this again influenced the way the Ottonian rulers understood their kingly rule.

From an artistic point of view, however, even more significant than the use which the royal family made of the humiliation of Christ is the fact that during this period Christians could produce a work of art as sublime as the Gero Crucifix, conveying at once a profound poignancy and a sense of the repose and serenity of God himself.

Archbishop Gero had himself been to Constantinople in order to escort to Cologne Princess Theophanu, who married Otto II. Theophanu was eventually buried in Cologne. This marriage was the occasion for the increase of Byzantine political, religious and artistic influence but it is a great puzzle to art historians as to exactly where this influence operated. Independently, in the West, there was a movement to recover antique and Carolingian models, the latter itself being a *Renovatio* of the late antique. After the end of iconoclasm, in 845, the period in Church history when there were fierce clashes between those who wished to destroy all images and those who regarded them as essential to the Christian faith, and the establishment of the new Macedonian dynasty in Constantinople, there was in the East also an attempt to recover the Christian Roman world. So both East and West were looking to Mediterranean models of late antiquity and it is not at all easy to work out where Byzantine influences lay and where the West was simply carrying through the programme begun by the Carolingians. No doubt Byzantine influence was an added spur to this recovery of the ancient Roman world artistically, as it certainly was politically and ceremonially, but the nature of that influence is difficult to trace in a scientific and systematic manner.

The Gero Crucifix has no parallel in the East at this time. However, we might at least suggest some artistic similarity in the way in which the body is shown in a graceful and, if one dare use the word, beautiful manner. The body of Christ in the mosaic at Hosios Loukas, described earlier, and dating from a little later than the Gero Crucifix, about 1020, is, as in other Byzantine depictions, not shown in a distorted or disfigured way. On the contrary, it still retains a dignity and grace. Similarly in the Gero Crucifix, as opposed to other depictions in the West, the body of Christ has grace as well as weight.

Although a strong artistic tradition developed in the Church in the East, there was always hostility to art in the round, because of its pagan associations. The Greco-Roman world had of course been full of statues of gods and goddesses and deified emperors. The pagan associations of this were too much for Christians, even after many centuries. In the West, in popular superstition evil spirits were meant to inhabit sculptures in the round. This is perhaps one of the reasons why Christian sculptures may have contained relics, to ensure that the power of the saint overcame any possible taint of evil. The Gero Crucifix is the oldest surviving example of a free-standing Christian sculpture in the West and it is remarkable for that alone. But it does not seem to have been used as a reliquary. Its purpose was simply to express and heighten devotion to the crucified Saviour, who for the sake of humanity became fully and truly human, even to painful death. The effect is not gruesome but utterly poignant.

Figure 12a: Volto Santo. Holy Face. Lucca, Cathedral

Christ Reigns from the Cross as Priest and King

— A Romanesque Carving of the Eleventh Century —

Around the middle of the eleventh century there emerged an artistic style which we now call Romanesque. Lasting until about 1200, the spread of the Romanesque style coincided with the flourishing of the great religious orders: the Cluniac, the Cistercian and the Carthusian. These monastic orders, enormously wealthy, built great churches and cathedrals in this new style.

Above all, the Romanesque period is known for its architecture. But the construction of churches was also accompanied by a great celebration of monumental sculpture which had been dormant for six hundred years due to its association with paganism. This for the most part consisted of relief sculpture in stone, subordinate to the architecture and placed in an overall framework provided by the building. Nevertheless, some fine free-standing carving in wood and metal was also produced.

Romanesque sculpture, with its semi-abstract style, has particularly appealed to people in the last hundred years. While Romanesque artists drew on the classical or Roman heritage, to our eyes they were not primarily concerned with depicting people in a natural style. There is very often a linear or abstract element in the work, which can give an appearance of calmness or severity, and sometimes great excitement. It appears that this element came from the abstract geometric decoration of the settled and converted Barbarian tribes who had moved into Northern Europe over the previous centuries; it was the fusion of these geometric elements with the remnants of the classical figurative tradition which provide the great appeal of Romanesque art.

The most striking form of crucifix in this period is one which shows Christ in triumph, reigning from the tree. He is depicted in a long-sleeved robe, with a distinctive knotted belt, rather than in a loin-cloth and half naked. The most famous image of that period, the so-called 'Volto Santo', which can still be seen at Lucca in Italy, is illustrated here. Legend says that this was carved by Nicodemus (it wasn't), but it was certainly well known by the eleventh century. This crucifix is not an isolated example. There are similar and in some ways even more striking versions of this in Catalonia, known there as 'Majestad'. Christ reigns from the Cross, his two feet separated and not nailed. As with the Volto Santo, they were painted.[31] Another recently restored crucifix of the Volto Santo type can be found in the Duomo of Borgo Sansepolcro dating to the ninth century.[32] The relationship between this, the one at Lucca and the 'Majestades' in Catalonia and their possible origin in Syria is a matter of discussion.

As discussed in the previous section, the image of the poignant, helpless Christ on the Cross began to appear in Germany in the tenth century. And, as we shall see, during the eleventh and twelfth centuries, major theological writers were stressing the suffering of Christ. This sense of Christ's suffering on the Cross was not lost in this Romanesque period. We see this, for example, in depictions of the Crucifixion where Christ is shown hanging, half naked, with his body sagging forward, but nevertheless with a crown on his head. There are a number of these crucifixes in metal in England. In Scandinavian countries, Christ is sometimes shown in this way but with more emphasis on the strength of Christ on the Cross, rather than his weakness.[33] At Langford in Oxfordshire, there are two relief carvings of the crucifix from this period. Both ilustrated here. One shows Christ in a long robe like the 'Volta Santo' at Lucca, though without the head. The other shows him half naked, in a loin-cloth, with head falling sideways but with something resembling a crown on his head, very like the metal crucifixes mentioned above. (Unfortunately the Victorian restorers of this carving re-assembled the arms the wrong way round).

There was a guild of merchants at Lucca who vied with those of Florence and Venice and it was from Lucca that the influence of the Volto Santo spread to England and elsewhere. Lucca was a major halt on the pilgrims' route from Canterbury to Rome, and small replicas of the image were made as souvenirs and as a focus of devotion. The Volto Santo image shows a sad and compassionate Christ. But here and in other depictions of the period it is above all the sense of majesty and dignity that is conveyed.

At the turn of the eleventh and twelfth centuries the Revelation of St John played an important role in the spiritual life of the time. Illuminated manuscripts and wall paintings represent John's vision in Chapter 1, with its description of the risen Christ as a high priest 'clothed with a long robe and with a golden girdle round his breast'. So the Christ on the Cross of Lucca is not only crucified but the one who will come in glory and who intercedes for us as priest and king.[34]

**Figure 12b: Christ on
the Cross in Long Robe
Langford, Oxfordshire**

**Figure 12c: Christ on
the Cross in a Loin-cloth
Langford, Oxfordshire**

Figure 13: *Halt at Emmaus*. Autun Cathedral

On the Road to Emmaus

— A Romanesque Relief of the Twelfth Century —

The scene in the Gospels where Christ walks as an unknown stranger with his two disciples on the road to Emmaus was not, so far as we know, depicted in early Christian art. It began to appear however when, instead of only one or two scenes being chose to witness to the risen Christ, artists under the patronage of the Church developed a whole cycle of Resurrection paintings. For example, in the twelfth-century Church of Panagia Chryselousa near Paphos in Cyprus, there is a cycle of twelve frescoes on the theme of the Resurrection dating from the fifteenth century. One of these depicts Christ on the road to Emmaus.[35] Painting in Cyprus in the fifteenth century was influenced by Western approaches as were the earlier mosaics at Monreale in Sicily. These magnificent mosaics have a number of depictions of the risen Christ appearing to his disciples, including one of the road to Emmaus, in which Jesus is depicted as a pilgrim, complete with stave. This is also how he is shown in Romanesque art is elsewhere in Europe in the twelfth century.

Mention was made in the previous section of the pilgrimage from Canterbury to Rome via Lucca. At that time, pilgrimages were an important part of life, particularly the one to Santiago de Compostela. In the cloister of Santo Domingo de Silos, on the pilgrim route in the north of Spain, Christ is shown with the cap and scrip (satchel) of a pilgrim. His legs are crossed to suggest motion and his feet are bare, an attribute in mediaeval carving of God or Christ, of angels or disciples. Interestingly, the Latin word *peregrinus* means both stranger and pilgrim and has very special application to the stranger/pilgrim who turned out to be the risen Christ. It also meant much to those mediaeval pilgrims, strangers in a foreign land, who on their journey and through their journey hoped to draw closer to that same risen Christ.

Shown here from Autun in France is a lively capital which was once thought to depict the healing of the blind man at Jericho. However, scholars are now clear that it refers to the moment in the Emmaus story where the disciples plead with Christ at the end of the day to come and eat with them. Again, Christ is shown as a pilgrim with his stave over his shoulder; the little figure on the right is an innkeeper opening the door to welcome Christ in.[36]

So although Christian depictions of the crucifixion and resurrection of Christ began with a few, basic images, the developing tradition allowed for further scenes. These scenes were taken from the Gospels but they were selected because of a particular resonance with their time. In the twelfth century, when pilgrimage was such a familiar and important feature of European life, it is not surprising that the Risen Christ should be depicted in terms of a pilgrim on the road to Emmaus.

Figure 14: The risen Christ appears to the two Marys. Mosaic from St Mark's Basilica, Venice

The Chairete

— A Venetian Mosaic of the Twelfth Century —

Matthew records an appearance of the risen Christ which no other Gospel mentions. He tells how Mary Magdalene and 'the other Mary' went to the Sepulchre and found it empty. As in Mark, an angel tells them that Jesus has gone before the disciples to Galilee: 'So they departed quickly from the tomb with fear and great joy, and ran to tell his disciples. And behold Jesus met them and said, "Hail!" And they came up and took hold of his feet and worshipped him. Then Jesus said to them, "Do not be afraid: go and tell my brethren to go to Galilee and there they will see me"' (Matthew 28:8–10). The Greek word for 'Hail', is 'Chairete', hence the name given to this appearance in Christian tradition.

As indicated in an earlier section, most figurative art in the East perished in the period of Iconoclasm from the seventh to the ninth centuries. A few depictions of the Chairete did however survive. For example, Dumbarton Oaks, the Byzantine study institute in Washington DC, holds four marriage rings dating from the mid-seventh century. Three of these depict the Myrophores but the fourth shows the Chairete. The Church of St Sergius at Gaza, which was built earlier than the year 536, also had a depiction of this scene, though this has not survived.[37] This image, part of the pre-iconoclastic tradition, was one that persisted until the middle Byzantine period in the East (843–1261) and which appears in the West until the Reformation.

The Chairete scene appears in two forms. The first depicts the women together and Christ addressing them. This, for example, is how the scene appears in the Rabbula Gospels, shown earlier (see p. 19).

The second example shows Christ standing between the two women and facing the viewer.[35] The two women, kneel at his feet. This is clearly an image which lends itself to devotion and can become as monumental and hierarchic as in the mosaic illustrated here from the Church of San Marco in Venice. To the right is the scene of doubting Thomas, while here on the left two tiny women kneel before a huge Christ.

Matthew refers to 'the other Mary' and it seems clear from an early reference that this is 'Mary the mother of James and Joseph', one of the women looking on the Crucifixion from afar. However, because of the reverence in which Mary the Mother of Jesus was held and the sense that it was appropriate for Christ to appear to his mother first, a tradition grew up in the Orthodox church that one of these women was in fact Mary the Mother of Jesus. Romanos, the great sixth-century poet, has a moving chapter on the appearance to Mary Magdalene. But in an earlier chapter on the lamentation of Mary the Mother of Jesus, when she meets her Son on the way to the Cross she is told, 'Courage, Mother because you will see me first on my coming from the tomb.'[36] This became established in the tradition of the Orthodox churches, though in fact the New Testament records no appearance to Mary the Mother of Jesus.

The wonderful mosaics of San Marco in Venice show strong Byzantine influence. Despite the vicissitudes of the relationship between Venice and Constantinople, there seems to have been a continuity of Byzantine craftsmen in the mosaic work of San Marco. This Chairete, though reflecting its twelfth-century original, has been restored a number of times.

Figure 15: *Crucifixion.* **The Amesbury Psalter**

The Influence of the Theologians

— A Thirteenth-Century Illuminated Gospel —

As already mentioned, an emphasis upon the suffering of Christ on the Cross began to develop in the West in the tenth century. This tendency was reinforced by the work of some great theologians in the eleventh and twelfth centuries. Anselm, who became Archbishop of Canterbury, dwelt with passionate intensity on the details of Christ's sufferings. As he wrote: 'Alas that I was not there to see the Lord of Angels humbled to the companionship of men ... Why, O my soul, wert thou not present to be transfixed with the sword of sharpest grief at the unendurable sight of your Saviour pierced with a lance, and the hands and feet of your Maker broken with the nails?'[40]

Previously, theologians had tended to think of the Crucifixion as a great conflict between God and the devil, with man as a helpless spectator in a cosmic drama. Anselm rejected that approach. He argued instead that God became man because only a human being could redeem humanity. Christians had often found it impossible to believe that the divine Son of God should be shown weak and suffering on the Cross. Indeed, this is raised to a fundamental theological objection in Islam and Judaism. But on Anselm's approach, the weakness and suffering of Christ on the Cross is an essential element. The Son of God became fully human in all aspects, sharing our suffering to the full, in order that he might redeem us. It was this emphasis upon the suffering of Christ on the Cross which was to increase its hold on European sensibility all through the next great period of art now usually labelled Gothic, which began in architecture in France in the early twelfth century and spread across Europe until it was superseded in Italy in the early fifteenth century though not until a century later in northern Europe.

Following Anselm, the great monk St Bernard of Clairvaux gave a more robust and integrated expression to such feelings. There was a surge of intense, ever-increasing religious emotion, which was spread by Bernard's Cistercians.

The influence of Anselm and Bernard was not of course the only one on this development. In Europe, blood was first depicted gushing from the right side of Christ in the late eighth century, in an illuminated manuscript in the Sacramentary of Gellone. As time went on, people began to meditate on this wound in the side of Christ as a door of grace to the heart of Jesus. This in turn led to the widespread devotion to the Sacred Heart, with its own feast. Devotion along these lines can be found in the work of St Bernard, as well as a number of thirteenth and fourteenth-century women mystics and saints, for example, St Mechtilde, St Gertrude and Julian of Norwich.

Another influence was the friar, St Francis of Assisi, who emphasised the suffering of Christ even before he experienced the Stigmata in 1224. He received in his own body the marks and wounds of Christ and this gave added impetus to devotion to the wounds of Christ.

In 1239 the French king, Louis IX, received what was claimed to be the Crown of Thorns from Constantinople. In fact, depictions of this crown indicate that it was a wreath of rushes. Before this time, the Crown of Thorns was not depicted; instead, Christ was shown crowned with a halo. Even in the thirteenth century, it was not the Crown of Thorns that we know but a wreath of rushes or a fillet of gold which only later, in the early fourteenth century, came to be depicted as a Crown of Thorns.[41]

Illustrated here is a depiction of the Crucifixion from the Amesbury Psalter, presently in All Souls College, Oxford.[42] It dates from about the year 1250 and has many of the characteristics of early Gothic manuscript illumination. The figures are elongated and graceful, there is powerful feeling but not of an exaggerated kind and there is some attempt at naturalism. Christ is shown half naked in a loin-cloth, with blood coming out of his wound, head on one side, eyes closed and arms and body hanging down. Round the head is a chaplet of rushes.

One of the features of this crucifix is the tree, with its ragged sawn-off branches. The Cross depicted as a tree has a long, rich history. Legend links the Cross on which Christ was crucified to the Tree of Life in the Garden of Eden and the Tree of Life described in Chapter 22 of the Book of Revelation. There are some beautiful poems and hymns on this theme as well as a rich variety of visual depictions. The identification of the Cross with Tree of Life was reactivated in the thirteenth century by the Meditations on the Cross of St Bonaventura. He described the Cross as a tree of leaves and flowers, which – as Revelation 22 says – bore fruit for Christians to eat.

So, as always, there were a number of factors shaping the mediaeval emphasis on the suffering of Christ but the influence of Anselm, Bernard and Francis was central. For, although their thought originated in monasteries or amongst the mendicant friars, such as the Franciscans, the religious orders which were so powerful at the time brought their intense devotion to the people as a whole. Ordinary Christian lay people felt they wanted to be with Christ at the foot of the Cross, entering into his suffering, and moved by it to love God with passionate intensity.

Figure 16: Crucifix by Cimabue in San Domenico, Arezzo

The Sublime Cimabue (1240–1302)

In the thirteenth century the Franciscan and Dominican religious orders were highly influential. Unlike the monastic orders such as the Cluniac, Cistertian and Carthusian, these were new orders, both founded in the thirteenth century, whose friars moved from place to place for preaching and ministering to urban populations. Both Franciscans and Dominicans in their different ways sought a religious revival and this resulted artistically in a rejection of extraneous decoration and a concentration on essentials. One of those essentials was the crucifix above the altar.

Three paintings of the Crucifixion by Cimabue have survived. Unfortunately, two of them are not in good order. The one on the walls of the upper church in Assisi has lost its original colouring while the one painted for the Franciscan Church of Santa Croce in Florence was severely damaged by floods, though a great deal of the power of that depiction still comes through. The painting stresses Christ's humanity, the body is less rigid and the background less sumptuous than the Crucifixion illustrated here. All details are played down and there are no golden highlights. Whilst Cimabue was still clearly influenced by Byzantine models, there is a new naturalism present, as a result of which he is usually placed, with Giotto, at the head of modern artistic developments.

The crucifix shown here is in the Church of San Domenico at Arezzo and was painted for the Dominicans.[43] It is rich and solemn, with a multi-coloured cloth background and gold leaf in the halo and on the highlights of the clothes.

The Dominicans stressed the rational order of the universe and they were in sympathy with artistic notions that this order should be reflected in art. But the rigidity of the square plan is softened in various ways, creating a scene of great spiritual power. The year 1260 had been predicted by Joachim of Fiore as the time of the end of the world. An apocalyptic fear gripped many people, intensifying religious devotion. It was around this time that Cimabue painted the crucifix, and the deepening shadows on the face of Christ may reflect the sombre mood of the times.

As discussed in earlier sections, by the early eleventh century Jesus was shown dead on the Cross both in the West (for example, in the Gero Crucifix in Cologne Cathedral, c. 975) and in the East (for example, in the mosaic in the church of Hosios Loukas, c. 1020). Nevertheless, during the thirteenth century there came an increasing emphasis in Italy on the depiction of Christ as *Christus Patiens*, rather than *Christus Triumphans*. This was significantly due to the influence of the Franciscans, who developed the whole cycle of stories on the Passion, as well as accentuating the suffering of Christ in depictions of the Crucifixion. The visual representation of this however was not just due to Franciscan meditations on that theme. The Franciscans had a wide range of contacts with the Byzantine world and the emphasis in Byzantine depictions of Christ on the Cross did not differ from Western depictions at this time as much as some have thought.[44]

In Italy, Scenes from the Passion had come to have a new dramatic quality, as, for example, in the Crucifixion panel on the pulpit in the Doumo in Siena by Nicola and Giovanni Pisano, father and son who sculpted mainly in the last part of the thirteenth century and very earliest part of the fourteenth. Duccio, who was active in the same period, had on the back of his great *Maesta* in Siena a number of Passion scenes, dominated by a dramatic representation, with the three crosses towering above two crowds, one weeping and mourning, the other angry and aggressive. For all its drama, this again reflects the strong Byzantine influence.[45] In contrast to these crowded scenes, Cimabue sets out a single, deeply moving image for contemplation.

Cimabue's is a suffering Christ, a depiction which by this time had firmly replaced the old triumphant understanding. Mary and John, traditionally shown at the foot of the Cross, are here shown at either end of the crossbar, mourning their Lord. They would have been familiar to onlookers from the 'Marian Lamentations', religious plays performed as part of the Good Friday liturgy from the thirteenth century onwards. Their mourning invites the onlooker to share with them in sadness.

Christ is shown with his head fallen on his shoulder, eyes closed. The expression is one of deep, inward concentration, attention and trust. Spiritually, he is already with his Heavenly Father, so the body, though suffering, also has a repose and serenity about it. Above all it is the face of Christ, in this Church of San Domenico, which even now stills the onlooker and kindles at least a flicker of that inward intensity.

Figure 17: *Noli Me Tangere* **by Giotto**

Noli Me Tangere

— Giotto's Masterpiece of the Early Fourteenth Century —

One of the most moving stories in the Gospels is the encounter of the risen Christ with Mary Magdalene in the garden. This story, which appears only in the Gospel of John, appears to indicate that Mary Magdalene was the first to see the risen Lord. However, this had theological difficulties. Would it not be more appropriate for the risen Lord to appear first to his mother? That, at any rate, is the natural tendency of both human feeling and religious devotion. Because of this and the growing emphasis upon the role of Mary, the Mother of Christ, Christians in the East were reluctant to depict the appearance to Mary Magdalene. They preferred to concentrate on the Chairete, where Mary Magdalene is one of the group of two or more women who encounter the risen Lord as they come away from the tomb. Moreover, as already mentioned in a previous section on the Chairete, there was a tendency to depict one of these women as Mary, the mother of the Lord. Depictions of Mary Magdalene on her own encountering Christ tend to be the result of Western influence, as for example on the Crusader façade of the Church of the Holy Sepulchre in Jerusalem.

In the West, there was less reluctance to single out Mary Magdalene, though it is uncertain how early the scene of her with the risen Christ was shown in art. There is a picture on the front of what is known as the Brescia Lipsanotheca, dating from 370, which shows a woman kneeling at the feet of Christ, who is shown unbearded and youthful and who stretches out his hand over her hand in a gesture of blessing. The distinguished art historian André Grabar thinks this is the earliest surviving example of the 'Noli me tangere' (Touch me not). However I am not convinced. Christ, far from turning away from her is looking towards her in a gentle compassionate way, with a gesture of blessing over her head.

With the growing cult of Mary Magdalene in the West, however, by Romanesque times there was no inhibition about depicting this scene and we have some superb examples of it, for example, on the cathedral door in Hildesheim, at Sauliu and in the cathedral at Autun. This Western tradition, in which Mary is shown reaching out to Christ, whilst he turns away in a gesture full of movement and meaning, found superb expression in a fresco by Giotto (1267–1337) in the Scrovegni Chapel in Padua shown here. In the chapel there are three main registers running all along the north and south walls and flanking the altar in the east. The sequence is easy to understand. The top register deals with the birth of Mary, drawn from the Apocryphal Gospels. The second and third registers tell the story of Christ's life, death and resurrection, and the scenes are based not only on the New Testament but a popular series of meditations on those New Testament scenes by a Franciscan *Meditationis Vitae Christi*, originally attributed to St Bonaventure. These meditations make the scenes human and accessible, encouraging the reader to enter imaginatively into them. The sequence goes from the Lamentation to the Ascension with the Noli Me Tangere as the only Resurrection scene in between. It is significant that the artist selected this scene to illustrate, rather than the more traditional ones of the women finding the tomb empty, or Christ appearing to Thomas.[46]

This Noli Me Tangere, shown here, has been called one of Giotto's most powerful images. On the left, the soldiers sleep, whilst above them the angels wait in the tomb. On the right, in a scene of dramatic intensity, Mary Magdalene reaches out to Christ with arms outstretched. He looks towards her with his right arm reaching out and his hand open, but his whole body is at the same time turning away from her. In this *contrapposto*, which has been defined as 'leaning towards her he also withdraws',[47] we have vivid artistic expression of the tension between the love of Mary Magdalene for Christ and his love for her and his desire to lead her into deeper truths.

Mary Magdalene was a highly popular figure in the West. *The Golden Legend*, written between 1255 and 1266 and translated into French in the fourteenth century, and which itself became a highly popular book, puts forward five reasons why Christ should have appeared first to Mary Magdalen. It says:

> For the first time he appeared to Mary Magdalene; as it is written in John, Chapter 20; and in Mark in the last chapter where it reads: 'But he rising early the first day of the week, appeared first to Mary Magdalene' (Mark 16:9); she signifies the repentant. But why he appeared first to her, for this there are five causes. The first is that she ardently loves; Luke 7:47 'Many sins are forgiven her because she hath loved much.' In addition he wished to show that he died for the sinners. Matthew 9:13. 'For I am not come to call the just, but sinners.' Thirdly he wanted to show that whores would get into the Kingdom of Heaven rather than the wise. Matthew 21:31 'I say to you that the publicans and the harlots shall

go into the Kingdom of God before you.' Fourthly: as a women as the announcer of the death, so a woman should also be an announcer of life, as the *Glossa* says. Fifthly, where sin has overflowed, so grace should be overflowing. Such as we read in Romans 5:20.[48]

These five reasons associate a number of stories in the Gospels with Mary Magdalene in a way which modern biblical scholars regard as unfounded. But it is easy to see how this combination of stories enhanced Mary Magdalene's popularity.

In the Arena Chapel in Padua, Mary Magdalene appears in three scenes: the Crucifixion, the Lamentation and the Resurrection. In each one, the arrangement of her hair is significant. Her light-coloured, flowing, abundant hair played an important part in the Gospel account of washing Christ's feet. In the Crucifixion scene, that same hair is shown flowing down her back. Although in the depiction of the Lamentation it is collected on her head, the hair is still prominent. In another depiction of the Noli Me Tangere scene, in the Church of St Francis in Assisi, which is probably in the tradition of Giotto rather than painted by Giotto himself, Mary Magdalene's hair is visible. In the Padua version however, some of the hair is covered and she wears unusual clothes, a large brown cloak over a pale dress. This was conventional dress for a mourner: only widows were to wear black, others to wear brown, though this brown could be of many different shades. So Mary Magdalene in this scene is shown with her hair, her glory, firmly covered, while her clothing indicates she comes as a mourner, though not as a widow.

The concept of *contrapposto*, or antitheses, was crucial in classical and Renaissance art. But for Christians, this had more than aesthetic significance. St Augustine quotes Paul, 'As poor yet making rich, having nothing yet possessing all things' and concludes, 'As, then, these oppositions of contraries lend beauty to the language, so the beauty of the course of this world is achieved by the opposition of contraries, arranged, as it were, by an eloquence not of words but of things.'[49] In this figure of Christ where all the forms of his figure are designed in sustained opposition we have, as I have said, tension between human love and divine desire. The outstretched hand of Christ is typical in its ambiguity, for it is both rejecting and blessing.

Figure 18: Lily Crucifix

A Lily Crucifix of the Late Fourteenth Century

During the fourteenth and fifteenth centuries, there developed in Europe a most unusual, haunting and beautiful depiction of the Crucifixion: Christ is shown crucified, not on a Cross, but on a lily.

The origin of this idea lies in the biblical conviction that Jesus was descended from Jesse, the father of King David. On the Sunday before Christmas, for example, the Old Testament reading contains the phrase from Isaiah 11:1: 'A shoot shall grow up from the stem of Jesse.' This idea received pictorial form in 'The Tree of Jesse'. Jesse is depicted lying on the ground and from his chest grows a branching tree or vine. On the branches are shown the descendents of Jesse, kings and prophets, up to Jesus. The Jesse Tree can be in stone, as in the tracery of a window in Dorchester Abbey in Oxfordshire, in glass or another medium. The Tree of Jesse seems to have emerged in the middle of the eleventh century in France.

Sometimes, on the apex of this tree is a lily and hanging on the flowers is Christ crucified. The relevant fact here is that 25 March, the Feast of the Annunciation, when Mary was told by an angel that she was going to give birth, was thought by people in mediaeval times also to be the day on which Christ was crucified. Hence as Mary, symbolised by a lily, conceived Christ on 25 March, so also on that day he is crucified, giving birth to our eternal life.

There are fifteen lily crucifixes in England.[50] Two are in Oxford, one in Queen's College and the other in the Church of St Michael-at-the-Northgate. Another, illustrated here, is in the Church of St Helen's, Abingdon, just a few miles south of Oxford. It has been suggested that this connection with Oxford is due to the theologian Duns Scotus, Duns the Scotsman (1264–1308). He was the first great theologian to defend the doctrine of the Immaculate Conception, which is the belief that Mary was conceived without original sin. This doctrine did not become Roman Catholic dogma until the nineteenth century but Pope Sixtus IV was voicing a groundswell of popular feeling when in 1476 he approved the Feast of the Immaculate Conception and its liturgical office.

The lily crucifix shown here is a particularly beautiful example. It was only fairly recently discovered and restored in St Helen's, Abingdon and dates from 1391. Christ is shown hanging dead, but there is not an undue emphasis on his suffering. Rather, there is a delicate beauty and repose about the depiction.

Figure 19a: The Anastasis. Kariye Mosque, Istanbul

The Anastasis

— A Fourteenth-Century Fresco —

An earlier section described the evolution of the Anastasis image and showed a mosaic from Daphni dating from around 1100. The fresco shown here is from the fourteenth century and is in the Chora Church (now the Kariye Mosque) in Istanbul. At that time the Byzantine Empire was reduced to virtually nothing. Nearly all Asia Minor had been lost and what remained was only a few hundred miles in what is now southern Bulgaria and parts of Greece. In 1453, even Constantinople itself was to fall and become a Muslim city. But this last beleaguered phase of the empire, under the Palaiologian dynasty, produced a beautiful late flowering of art, of which the mosaics and frescoes in the Chora Church are an outstanding example.

Art historians distinguish four types of the Anastasis image.[51] Shown here is the fourth type, the last to evolve. Its distinguishing feature is that Christ is shown pulling both Adam and Eve from the abode of the dead.

To the left of the fresco is John the Baptist, pointing at Christ, and the kings David and Solomon, indicating Christ's human descent. To the right of the picture Eve is being pulled clear of the sarcophagus, whilst behind her is a new figure, a young man holding a crook. This is Abel, the shepherd, killed by his brother Cain; Abel begins to appear in the Anastasis from the eleventh century onward. Writings from this time reveal why he was included. He is the first human being to be killed, an innocent person, whose blood cries out to God. In a series of complex parallels and contrasts, Abel and Christ are juxtaposed. For example, whereas the blood of Abel intercedes, the blood of Christ redeems.

In early depictions of the Anastasis Adam is shown alone. Then Eve begins to appear behind him, reflecting Eve's secondary role in creation and the Fall. Here, however, Eve is on a par with Adam, both being raised together. Homilies of the time say that as Eve was taken from the side of Adam, creating a wound, so the wound in Christ, the new Adam, heals that pain and redeems womankind as well.

The presence of Abel and Eve together is also of significance. For Abel was of course the son of Eve. As Eve gave birth to Abel, so Mary, the new Eve, gave birth to the new Adam who would redeem mankind. In fact without Abel's birth there would have been no descent of Christ, so that birth is a key element in the salvation of humanity:

> The blood of the righteous shepherd Abel, the son of Eve, intercedes for mankind, while the blood of Christ, the Son of Mary, the blessed daughter of Eve, ransoms mankind. So Eve, the mother of Abel, is anti-type as well as the ancestor of the Virgin Mary. Through the inclusion of Abel, the child-bearing ability of Eve is offered indirectly as guarantee of her salvation.[52]

In this fresco, which is in the apse of the Cemetery Chapel of the Chora Church, there is an equal emphasis on Christ himself in the centre facing the viewer and Adam and Eve whom he is raising from the dead. Beneath Christ's feet are the bars and keys of Hell and the bound figure of Hades; however, the emphasis is not on his defeat but on Christ's resurrecting power. Christ is surrounded by a mandorla (which literally means almond) of light, which in this case is spangled. The three layers of light symbolise the Trinity. During the fourteenth century, particularly in the work of the theologian Gregory Palamas, there was great emphasis on the uncreated light of God. This light shone in Jesus when he was transfigured before the three disciples, Peter, James and John, on the mountain (Luke 9:28–36). Here that same uncreated light shines in darkest Hell.

The other noteworthy feature of this magnificent icon is the way that Adam and Eve seem to float free. They are about to join Christ in a joyous dance of life, the life that has overcome all evil and death.

Figure 19b: The Anastasis. Kariye Mosque, Istanbul

Figure 20: *The Man of Sorrows*

The Man of Sorrows (c. 1490)

This engraving by Israhel van Meckenem, made about 1490, is not to the taste of most people today. But this type of devotional image, *The Man of Sorrows*, has been described as the most precise visual expression of late mediaeval piety, bringing image and viewer together with a religious intensity that has rarely been surpassed.[53]

There was an earlier, simpler form of *The Man of Sorrows*, which consisted simply of Christ's head and shoulders, with the eyes shut and head inclined to one side. The few known examples are all from the Byzantine period. These images were used for private devotion, usually as part of a Triptych: the image of Christ in the centre, with that of the Virgin of Sorrows folding over it and the image of a sorrowing John the Baptist folding over both of them. Such triptychs could easily be carried by monks on their travels.

The more usual form of *The Man of Sorrows* was like the one here, a half-length figure of the suffering Christ in front of the Cross with arms folded on his breast. A mosaic icon of this type, produced in Constantinople around 1300, was taken to the Church of Santa Croce in Gerusalemme, in Rome. This image was of central importance for devotion in both East and West, expressing and evoking intense religious devotion. A Franciscan prayer book made in Genoa around 1300 identifies the prayers that were said in the West before the Byzantine image of *The Man of Sorrows*. One reads, 'O how intensely thou embraced me, good Jesu, when the blood went forth from thy heart, the water from thy side, the soul from thy body. Most sweet youth, what hast thou done that thou should'st suffer so? Surely I, too, am the cause of thy sorrow.'[54]

Such prayers were also attributed to St Bernard of Clairvaux, who greatly influenced this type of devotion. The National Gallery in London now has, united, a fine example of this icon dating from 1260, together with the other part of the diptych, showing Mary sharing in the suffering of her son, thus providing an example to believers to do the same.[55]

This icon became popular in the West due to the efforts of the Carthusians of Santa Croce, where the icon was kept. They wanted to publicise their church and so made the icon the centre of their campaign. They approached Israhel van Meckenem, the best-known printmaker of the day, to make an engraving of the icon, together with a smaller version for those of more modest means. This brings out another crucial feature of late mediaeval art, namely, that it was not only the vehicle for intense devotion, but for a devotion which spread widely through the population as a whole through engravings and woodcuts. In the period 1300 to 1500 religious art ceased to be a purely public matter. Images were present in people's homes and went with them on their travels. Very often someone who commissioned a work of religious art would have their own image, worshipping Christ, incorporated into the picture. Religious manuals encouraged the supplicant to imagine that they were actually present in the scene, holdling the Christ Child or suffering with the adult Christ.

In the West, this particular image of *The Man of Sorrows* gained even more prestige because it was alleged that the image of Christ had come in a vision to the great Pope Gregory (540–604). It was in any case regarded as a *vera icon*, a true icon, because anything that had come from Constantinople was regarded as authentic. But, more importantly it was believed that the image originated in the sixth century and had been authorised by Pope Gregory himself, who when saying Mass had had revealed to him a natural portrait of Christ which was recorded in the mosaic prototype. The fact that this revelation came to Pope Gregory during the Eucharist helped to reinforce belief in the real presence of Christ in the sacraments.

Another factor encouraged the spread of this image and the devotion associated with it, namely the sale of indulgences. The sale of indulgences was fundamental to mediaeval religious life and it was from the money so raised that hospitals, hostels and churches were built and works of art commissioned. Thus prayers said before the icon, whether in the form of a portable diptych or triptych, or engraving, would help the believer through the period of purgation that preceded heaven.

The Man of Sorrows is an image for pure contemplation. It is the simple image of Christ in his suffering, not associated with any other scenes from the Passion cycle. It said to the person praying in front, 'See how much I suffer for you, see how much I love you.' The person praying would be inspired to respond in a similar vein, with an answering love and a desire to share in the suffering of Christ. As has been written:

New emotional qualities characterise the Western Man of Sorrows; they are intimacy, compassion, exaltation and intercession. So direct is his confrontation with the spectator that the suffering Son of God and the sinful man seek one another in their love. Christ who has mercy on mankind himself implores mercy: 'Have done thou'. Yet this entreaty is also an admonition from him who is the judge.[56]

Figure 21: *Resurrection* by Piero della Francesca

Christ Rises from the Grave

— Piero della Francesca's Humanist Vision of the Fifteenth Century —

As was indicated in earlier sections, Christian artists for the first thousand years of the Church's history showed great reluctance to probe the actual mystery of Christ rising from the grave. They depicted either the women arriving at the tomb and finding it empty, or the Anastasis, a symbolic rendering of Christ's triumph over evil and death. There were a few attempts to show Christ's actual rising but they are very few and they did not catch on. By the twelfth century however this had changed. The idea of showing Christ's bodily resurrection was more generally accepted, though the scene was less common in Italy. The exception to this is the fresco by Piero della Francesca (1410/20–92) shown here. It can be seen in the town museum in Sansepolcro, where this and other murals in fresco and tempera have been carefully preserved and well displayed. Although Christian believers today tend to find Piero's depiction of the rising of Christ too literalistic, paradoxically the picture has great appeal to some agnostics. Aldous Huxley for example described it without qualification in an essay as 'the best picture in the world'. For him it expressed the humanist ideal, hence the use of the word 'humanist' in the title of this section.

Piero della Francesca absorbed the Florentine advances in perspective, together with its recovery of classical symmetry and drew them together in a unified, refined and complete way. The basis of his painting was a geometric, mathematical precision, combined with clear lines and a great feeling for the cool, crystalline daylight of Tuscany, resulting in paintings characterised by an extraordinary, almost haunting clarity, dignity and order.

As the name of the town, then called Borgo Sansepolcro, recalls, legend related its foundation to the Holy Sepulchre in which Christ was buried and it may have had a stone which its citizens claimed to be from that site. This, together with a traditional painting of the rising of Christ in the town, made it an obvious scene for Piero della Francesca.

In this picture the vertical dimension is emphasised by trees and the

banner held by Christ. This is intersected by the horizontals: the streaks of
cloud in the sky, the lid of the sarcophagus and its base. But this is no boring
symmetry, because the lance of the soldier as well as the soldiers' lolling
heads and the robes of Christ intersect the more rigid verticals and
horizontals to provide a different kind of balance and interest.

The light in this picture is particularly effective. It is the light of dawn in
the sky picking out the white body of Christ and the faces of the sleeping
soldiers – an early, unearthly light. There may also be some obvious
symbolism, because the tree to the left of Christ is bare while the trees on
the right are evergreen cypresses. These are set within the landscape that was
familiar to Piero, near Borgo Sansepolcro.[57]

Christ faces us, in majesty, with the traditional banner of the Resurrection
indicating triumph over death. Below him the soldiers sleep, and one in
particular, perhaps a self-portrait of Piero della Francesca, could almost be
dreaming the whole scene. The wound remains in Christ's body, but the
flesh is beautiful and the body classical in proportion. This is why Aldous
Huxley admires the painting:

> The being who rises before my eyes from the tomb is more like a Plutarchian
> hero than the Christ of conventional religion. The body is perfectly developed,
> like that of a Greek athlete; so formidably strong that the wound in his muscular
> flank seems somehow an irrelevance. The face is stern and pensive, the eyes
> cold. The whole figure is expressive of physical and intellectual power. It is the
> resurrection of the classical ideal, incredibly much grander and more beautiful
> than the classical reality, from the tomb where it had lain so many hundred
> years.[58]

When my wife looked at this picture however, it was a different aspect
which drew her. The eyes of Christ are those of a man who has gone through
crucifixion and death. Nevertheless, the experience of crucifixion and death
in this risen Christ is not nearly as marked as in the one painted by a near
contemporary, the Milanese artist Bartolomeo Suardi Bramantino
(1465–1530) which is now in the Thyssen-Bornemisza collection in Madrid.

The body of Bramantino's Christ, still partially swathed in its white
winding sheet and bathed in moonlight, has a pale, unearthly pallor – except
for the wounds which Christ displays and his face and reddish hair in
shadow. The eyes, bloodshot with tears, stare directly at the viewer. This
Christ still bears the marks of death; it is perhaps the most haunting painting
of the risen Christ ever painted.

By contrast, as Huxley observed, Piero's Christ looks set to live a fully human life on the human stage: in fine shape, in every sense of that word. The contrast of Bramantino and Piero brings out the impossibility of depicting the mysterious truth that the Church has proclaimed at this point: a Christ who has both died and overcome death for all people for all time.

Figure 22: Detail from Christ on the Cross. The Isenheim Altarpiece by Matthias Grünewald

Extreme Agony

— The Isenheim Altarpiece —

The altarpiece for the monastery at Isenheim in Alsace was painted by the artist we know as Matthias Grünewald (1460–1528). Grünewald was, with Dürer, the most popular German painter of his time though, by the nineteenth century, his work was hardly discussed. The change in the way the painting was perceived can be pinpointed quite accurately and dramatically to when it was taken from Colmar to be shown in Munich for a year during 1918/19.[59] The altarpiece, and the art books and photographs promoting it, promulgated and reinforced a German self-image which saw in Grünewald – as well as later, twentieth-century German expressionism – the idea of an anguished, martyred, angst-ridden people. During the twentieth century this self-image, originally contextualised at a particular point in German history, began to have a much wider resonance, particularly in Europe as a whole, as people became ever more conscious of the suffering and tragedy of human existence. The distinguished art historian Jane Dillenberger has called this painting, 'A work of such tremendous and dismal grandeur of expression that nothing on earth seems to equal it'.[60] And the theologian Paul Tillich named it the greatest German picture ever painted. Our experience of suffering over the last hundred years, particularly in two terrible world wars, draws us to the thought of a God who shares our human suffering and leads us to the artistic expression of such a belief. Similarly, the time when this picture was painted, about 1515, was also extremely turbulent. Although Grünewald's work was commissioned by archbishops, he was involved in the Peasants' Revolt and drawn towards Lutheranism, though he never actually became a Lutheran. Many people had expected the end of the world in the year 1500 and this heightened the atmosphere for years afterwards.

An even more important factor for the understanding of this painting is that it was painted for the Order of St Anthony, who tended the sick, particularly those afflicted with St Anthony's fire or ergotism, a disease causing horrific lesions and eruptions of the skin. A new patient was brought first before the altarpiece in the chapel in the hope of a cure through direct divine intervention. If such a miracle did not occur, the patient at least had the consolation of knowing that Christ's sufferings were like his. In the painting, Christ's flesh is shown torn by whips, whilst the birches used for the flagellation have left splinters embedded in his flesh. The Crown of Thorns is no pretty adornment but consists of long sharp spikes which dig into the head and body. The body is taut, with the skin stretched and a gaping wound is visible. Every detail of the painting seems to accentuate the sense of agony. Even the great crossbeams bend under the tension of the body. The fingers of Christ claw stiffly at the empty air while his head sags lifelessly in the hollow created by shoulder muscles torn from their sockets. Similarly, the ankle bones are riven from their sockets as the weight of the body is pressed down upon them.

Grünewald achieves his effects partly by an asymmetrical balancing of the forms in the painting. For example, the crucifix is to one side of the fold in the centre of the panel. No less important is the way the artist uses line, in a restless, highly expressive way. Indeed he has been called a forerunner of twentieth-century German expressionism, and, as mentioned earlier, German writers after the First World War believed that both expressed the essential German spirit.

Another important influence on this picture was the writings of St Bridget. Bridget was a Swedish woman who founded a religious order, now known as the Bridgettines. A woman of intense personality, she claimed religious visions, which she dictated in a book of revelations, chiefly about Christ's sufferings. Her description of Christ's sufferings closely resembles Grünewald's painting.

Grünewald's great painting is made up of a number of hinged panels. When the polyptych is closed, the crucifixion scene is visible. When open, there are a number of scenes on the inside, culminating in a startling resurrection with the colours bright red and orange predominating; and Christ rises in a circle of light above the tomb and the guards, against a background of a starry sky. The predella below portrays the entombment.

In the Crucifixion scene itself, on the left, Mary Magdalene rises in agony and Mary the mother of Jesus swoons, while to the right there is the somewhat unusual depiction of John the Baptist at the Crucifixion pointing to Jesus with the Latin inscription from John 3:30 by his side 'He must increase, but I must decrease'. At his feet is the lamb of God, holding a cross, the lamb bleeding into a chalice. Christ is the lamb of God sacrificed for the sins of the world – his blood, shed for our forgiveness, can be received in the Eucharist.[61]

This portrayal of Christ shows him in sheer agony: mouth open, eyes closed and brow furrowed, stomach drawn in to the spinal column, the flesh dreadfully marked. However extreme the suffering of those in the monastic hospital, they knew that Christ was with them in their agony and he would sustain them through the sacrament of the Eucharist. This idea was not new. In the Basilica of S. Julien, at Brioude in the Auvergne is a large fourteenth-century carved figure of Christ in polychrome wood. This is the so-called 'Leprous Christ' because of the disfigurement of the face and figure. It is from the former leper house at Bajasse and is thought to have been carved by an inmate, with all the knowledge of the suffering which the disease entailed. The Christ of Grünewald's Isenheim Altarpiece expresses, in the most brutally realistic way, the conviction that God himself in Christ experiences the violence of human life, of which people in the sixteenth century and the twenty-first century were and are so conscious.

Figure 23: *The Supper at Emmaus* by Michelangelo M. da Caravaggio

The Supper at Emmaus

— By Caravaggio in the Seventeenth Century —

Michelangelo Merisi da Caravaggio (1573–1610) lived a short and tempestuous life. In 1606 he had to flee from Rome, where he was working, after killing a man in a brawl. For four years he wandered between Naples, Malta and Sicily before dying of malaria at the age of 37. His dramatic paintings were also highly controversial in their time. Sometimes, his commissions for religious paintings were refused upon completion because they looked at old subjects in a new way. Caravaggio tried simply to show the truth as he saw it, devoid of idealised forms of beauty. He was condemned as a 'naturalist', the first artist to be disparaged in a slogan.

In his painting of Doubting Thomas, the disciples, depicted very much like old labourers and common people, are peering and poking about at Christ's wound in a very crude manner. In the painting *The Supper at Emmaus*, illustrated here, there is a similar realism. The apples are bruised, the disciples wear worn clothes and their features are coarse.

The moment when the disciples recognise the stranger in the midst as the risen Christ is shown in a dramatic way, with arms outstretched and astonished faces. Here as elsewhere Caravaggio achieves part of his effect by the use of brilliantly lit figures against a dark background. The light is coming from behind the viewer, illuminating the face of Christ, which in turn seems to light up part of the faces of the two disciples. But, if it is physical light that unifies the objects and people in the painting in one way, then, as John Drury has written:

> There supernatural or inward integration is achieved by the Mass itself. For it holds together inanimate and animate nature – food, utensils and people – in the mystery of Christ's presence which permeates both and gathers them into one … *The Supper at Emmaus* is a fusion of epic theatre and domestic still life. It has a high-definition and homeliness and high drama, held together by Christ's blessing of food. This is decidedly and completely the Mass – and the archetype of all subsequent celebrations of it. Held in this moment of transubstantiation of inert matter by energetic spirit, Caravaggio can show a community of strongly

differentiated and individual people and, like a priest at the altar, invite the spectator into it. The individuality and community of sacrament mark it everywhere.[62]

The Supper at Emmaus was not a well-known scene in the first thousand years of Christian art but it began to appear more frequently in Romanesque and Renaissance times. During the period of the Reformation and the Counter-Reformation, the place and meaning of the Eucharist was a crucial debate. It is not surprising therefore that at this time the scene of the Supper at Emmaus, which has Eucharistic overtones, should be of importance. For in the Gospel story in the supper at Emmaus Jesus 'Took the bread and blessed and broke it and gave it to them' – actions that replicate those at the last supper. The story continues: 'And their eyes were opened and they recognised him' (Luke 24:30–31). Paintings of this scene would reinforce Catholic belief that Christ was truly present in the Eucharist. It was a scene painted not only by Caravaggio but a little later by Rembrandt. Caravaggio puts before the viewer a moment of great drama and intensity. The onlooker can feel that they are there, at the table, in this flash of recognition. One feature that John Drury draws attention to is the way the basket of fruit seems about to topple over the edge of the table. Our domestic instinct is to reach forward to steady it:

> This genially trivial trespassing beyond the picture plane (not unprecedented) is matched by more profound ones, impelled by the sudden recognition of Jesus in his blessing of the bread. The man on the left pushes his chair back at us with involuntary force. The man on the right throws his arms aside with such abandoned amazement that his left hand seems to break through the bounds of the picture space and come out into the air between him and us. These effects are irresistible and famous and seem to put us in the path of the oncoming vehicle of Christ's actions; but they have a serious function which is less often noticed. The pushed chair and wide gesture are conductors of revelation. They carry Christ's self-declaratory gesture out into the spectators world as urgently as the poised basket of fruit invites every spectator into the company within.[63]

Figure 24: *Christ on the Cross* by Rembrandt

Jesus Alone

— Rembrandt —

For the first part of his life Rembrandt van Rijn (1606–69) painted in a grand, dramatic manner. Then, in the early 1640s, he experienced great suffering, including debt, and the death of his three children and his wife Saskia. His style changed and he focused henceforth on the ordinary, human faces of the people about him, with Christ almost hidden in their midst.

This painting was done in 1631, when Rembrandt was 35, at a time in his artistic development when he wished to convey the full force of the biblical narrative in a dramatic manner. Because of the nature of the subject, his early style seems to come into its own in this painting, for Rembrandt powerfully conveys the moment when Jesus cried out, 'My God, my God, why hast thou forsaken me?' Most of the painting is dark, indeed black. Nearly all the light is on the body of Jesus nailed to the Cross, with only a faint, hazy glow in the sky at the top of the frame.

This portrayal of Jesus, alone on the Cross, only became popular in the seventeenth century. Before this time, it was usual to show other people present. Initially, only John, the beloved disciple, and Mary, the mother of Jesus, were present in a most characteristic and austere depiction in the East, but in the fifteenth and sixteenth centuries, particularly in the West, the Crucifixion became an increasingly crowded and dramatic scene. In the seventeenth century, however, a number of artists decided to focus simply on Jesus on the Cross with no other figure present. Rubens painted one crucifixion scene like this as did the Spanish painters Zurbaran, Murillo and, in a very famous portrayal, Valasquez. This Spanish tradition was continued by Goya in his depiction of the crucifixion scene in 1780. Rembrandt has given the scene his personal stamp through his powerful use of chiaroscuro – the relationship between light and dark in a painting – and his realistic technique. The eye is drawn to the anguish in Christ's face as he cries out. The parchment above his head, on which were written the words 'Jesus of Nazareth, the King of the Jews' in Hebrew, Greek and Latin, uneven and curling at the edges, seems very real. The same attention to detail is shown in the wood of the Cross, the crossbar scraped bare but the bottom of the upright with some of its bark still attached.

It was only in 1959 that Rembrandt's signature and the date 1631 were discovered on the painting. Rescued from oblivion and carefully examined, it may possibly have been designed as the centrepiece for three works, between the erection of the Cross on one side and the descent from the Cross on the other. We do know that in 1805 the painting was bought at an auction in Dunkirk and donated to the parish church of Le Mas D'Agenais. It is the only religious work by Rembrandt which now hangs in a church.[64] There is a poignancy, as well as drama about this picture: it was painted right at the beginning of Rembrandt's career, when all looked so promising; nevertheless, he was able to enter imaginatively into the anguish and loneliness of Jesus of the Cross. During the course of his life, suffering became very much a reality for him and it is not surprising that he returned to the theme of the Cross to produce some of his most powerful and best-known drawings and etchings.

Figure 25: *Morning in the Riesengebirge by Caspar David Friedrich*

Caspar David Friedrich and the Cross in Landscape

Though the eighteenth century produced many fine portrait painters there is little religious art from that period which appeals to us today. All this began to change at the end of the eighteenth century and in the early part of the nineteenth with what came to be called the Romantic Movement. Like all artistic categories the Romantic Movement has blurred edges but artists of this time shared a reaction against what they thought of as the shallow rationalism of the Enlightenment. They wanted to go, as they felt, deeper into the nature of things. Eighteenth-century painters had sought the sublime in nature but to the Romantics their picturesque scenes had no hint of 'inner goings-on' as Coleridge put it. Romantic artists looked for 'Something far more deeply interfused'. The result is that romantic landscapes often have a strongly religious quality to them.[65] Constable, for example, was a religious person who sought to respond to the truth of the divine in landscape. He and others transferred to landscape something of the Protestant attitude to God. Sometimes these landscapes are manifestly symbolic, as those depicted by Caspar David Friedrich, which have an ambivalent, hallucinatory quality. Though they are full of symbols, their power does not rest simply in the symbols but in the 'strong intense polarity of closeness and distance, precise detail and sublime aura'. Not surprisingly the Romantic Movement has been termed 'Spilt Religion' and the second part of a major book on Caspar David Friedrich is entitled 'Art as Religion'.[66] These works from the Romantic Movement reveal a sense of the solitariness of the artist and the isolation of the viewer (or listener), an isolation related to the sundering of bonds of community by a rapidly industrialising society. The artist's life, his subjectivity, his feelings, all come strongly to the fore.

One of Caspar David Friedrich's most famous works, *Cross in the Mountains*, was commissioned as an altarpiece. The firs and the Cross silhouetted against the sky evoke a sense of a lonely soul reaching out to the infinite. The rays of light shining out from behind the mountain and the colour of the sky indicate new hope, fresh start, resurrection. The less well-known work, *Morning in the Riesengebirge*, reproduced here, painted in 1810, has the same effect in a less obvious way. Most people love mountains and for many, mountains have an awesome, religious quality. Even without the Cross in this picture, the mountain range, bare and austere in the forefront and misty in the background, would evoke a strange admixture of feelings of closeness and distance, longing and satisfaction. The slim silhouette of the Cross, with a tiny figure leaning against it, is not alien to this landscape. On the contrary, it focuses its religious appeal in Christian terms. The infinite for which humans long, evoked by such landscapes, is nothing less than the beauty of love given to the uttermost. The God who gives us the rocks gives us his crucified Son. And both draw us out of ourselves to wonder and worship.

Figure 26: *White Crucifixion* **by Marc Chagall**

The White Crucifixion

— Marc Chagall —

Marc Chagall (1887–1985) was born in the Russian town of Vitebsk, of Jewish parents. He lived through the tumultuous times of the twentieth century, close both to its suffering and its artistic developments. After studying in Russia he joined the group of avant-garde artists who lived in Paris before the First World War. After the Russian Revolution, he benefited from the opening up of society to Jews and for a time ran an art school. However, this did not last and he returned to France until forced to flee the Nazis in 1942. During the Second World War, he lived in the United States before returning to live in the south of France for the last seventeen years of his life. His art has reflected some of the main artistic trends of the twentieth century: Cubism, the Russian avant-garde, German Expressionism and Surrealism. But all his work is imbued with its own highly distinctive character. His lyrical inner vision, drawing on the Jewish life and Hasidic insights of his youth, expressed in joyous colour and floating figures, are unmistakable.[67]

Chagall painted *The White Crucifixion* in 1938 after he had travelled in Europe and experienced the rise of Nazi brutality. In June 1938, the first transport of Jews, numbering around 1500, were taken to the concentration camps; in that month and in August synagogues in Munich and in Nuremberg were destroyed and pogroms carried out. The picture was originally even more specific then it is now, for before over-painting, the old man at the lower left-hand side had 'Ich bin Jude' (I am a Jew) written on the plaque which he wears round his neck. The painting shows in vivid details, in an iconic way, the destruction of the closed but joyous Jewish world he had known in Russia as a child. At the bottom of the Cross is the Menorah, the seven-branch candlestick of Judaism, though here with only six candles and only five alight. Then in an anti-clockwise direction, a mother hugs her child to her chest as she flees the destruction. Above her is a Torah scroll with white light streaming from it and a figure stepping over the light. This refers to a famous Hasidic tale, when a bishop ordered the

Torah to be burnt. Rabbi Israel prayed and his prayers pierced to the palace of the Messiah. As a result the Bishop fell into a fit, which frightened those who intended to burn the scrolls. A white light from the scroll, symbolising the Word of God, spreads to the Cross and is traversed by a green-clad figure carrying a bundle. This figure appears in a number of Chagall's paintings. He has been interpreted as the Jewish wanderer of Yiddish tradition, shown begging due to the hardship and pogroms imposed on his people. But there is also a more optimistic interpretation, in which the figure is seen as Elijah, who in times of tribulation brings help, appearing in all kinds of disguises. It would seem to be primarily Elijah to whom Chagall is referring in his autobiography when he describes the custom of the Day of the Atonement of opening the doors to let in the prophet Elijah in the words:

> But where is Elijah in his white chariot?
> Is he still waiting in the courtyard, perhaps, to enter the house in the guise of a wretched old man, a hunchback beggar, with a pack on his back and a stick in his hand?
> 'Here I am, where is my glass of wine?'

Above Elijah a synagogue is being burnt by a Nazi brownshirt, whilst behind Nazi flags can be seen. The sacred furniture and books have been thrown out into the street. Above the door are two lions, which often appear in Eastern European synagogues, though here there may also be a personal reference, for Chagall's first name Marc has, in Christian symbolism, the lion as his image.

At the top of the painting, Jewish figures lament and flee while on the left of the picture, a Jewish *shtetl* (village) is burnt by Communist troops with red flags. Flames flare from the roofs and the homeless sit on the ground outside. Below this scene there are some trying to escape in a boat – to Palestine. At the bottom left, Jewish figures clutching the sacred scrolls run from the destruction.

Dominating the picture in the centre is the figure of Christ crucified. But this is very much a Jewish Christ. Over his head written in Hebrew are the words 'King of the Jews', whilst round his body is wrapped a Jewish prayer shawl. A great shaft of white light comes down from Heaven and a ladder is propped against the Cross. The ladder, the ladder of Jacob's vision reaching to Heaven, was a favourite motif of Chagall and appears in a number of his paintings. He once wrote a poem on the subject:

> Lying down like Jacob asleep
> I have dreamed a dream
> An angel seizes me and hoists me up on the ladder
> The souls of the dead are singing.

It is truly remarkable that at the centre of this painting is the figure of Jesus on the Cross: the suffering of the Jewish people is summed up in a Christian icon. The agony of Jesus is seen as the agony of all Jewish people. Chagall painted the crucified Christ in a number of his paintings, even one of the Exodus. This is startling, even shocking when we remember that for many Jews the Cross has been a symbol of Christian oppression of Jewish people. Many Jews have, quite understandably, felt very uneasy about Chagall's paintings that incorporate the Crucified One. It is also difficult to see how, in the light of the Holocaust and our greater awareness of how traditional Christian anti-Judaism prepared the way for it, any Jew today could use this symbol. But Chagall did and he was not alone amongst Jews of his time. The most important sculptor in Russia at the turn of the century was a Jew, Marc Antokolsky, whose letters reveal how he struggled to reconcile Jewish and Christian viewpoints. Antokolsky accepted Jesus in the line of biblical prophets and welcomed the love which he believed he showed, without accepting the doctrinal tenets of the Christian religion. When Chagall was studying in St Petersburg, it was hoped by his Jewish patrons that he would become a second Antokolsky. In one of his letters Antokolsky wrote:

> For several weeks now I have been working on 'Christ', or as I call him, 'Great Isaiah'. Jews may have renounced him, but I solemnly admit that he was and died as a Jew for truth and brotherhood ... The Jews think I'm Christian and the Christians curse me for being a dirty Jew (*Zhid*). The Jews rebuke me: 'Why did I do Christ', and the Christians rebuke: 'Why did I do Christ like that?'[68]

What is perhaps most remarkable about Chagall's painting is his use of white: the white light coming from the flames of the burning Torah, mingling with the white shaft coming from Heaven onto the Cross and suffusing the whole picture. From one point of view this is smoke, all part of terrible conflagration and destruction. But it is also the white light of the Torah, the eternal Word of God which stands through all things. There is a stillness in the centre, focused on the figure on the Cross, which the terrible scenes cannot destroy. From a Christian point of view, that figure on the Cross is God himself sharing in the agony of his people during the terrible events of the Nazi period. From Chagall's point of view, in this incredibly brave Jewish use of Christian imagery, this is a symbol of Jewish faithfulness to the Torah even in the midst of utter destruction, a faithfulness which stands forever, because it is founded on God's word.

Figure 27: *Christ on the Cross* by Georges Rouault

Christ on the Cross

— Georges Rouault —

Rouault (1871–1958) was early apprenticed to a stained-glass maker but he soon found himself studying with the leading artists of the time, especially Matisse. Rouault was hostile to the approach of the Impressionists, but nor did he seek to produce a representational art. In so far as he fits into any of the artistic labels of the time he is best described as an Expressionist, seeking non-representational images to express strong inner feeling. As he put it:

> Art, the art I aspire to, will be the most profound, the most complete, the most moving expression of what man feels when he finds himself face to face with himself and with humanity. Art should be a disinterested, passionate confession, the translation of the inner life, as it used to be in the old days in the hands of our admirable anonymous Frenchman who sculpted the figures on the cathedrals.[69]

Gustave Moreau, the teacher to whom Rouault remained devoted, died in 1898 and as a result Rouault had a major breakdown, at once physical, emotional and spiritual. Although he believed his style became lighter when he recovered, in fact the dark lines in Rouault's pictures are one of its distinguishing features. They convey a sense of sombre suffering, the tragedy of life, which never left him. Rouault became a devout Catholic, was influenced by a number of Catholic literary figures of the time and. at one stage, wished to form a monastic community with other Catholic artists. Although the Roman Catholic Church failed to commission any of his works, all his paintings, not just the ones on religious themes, have a profoundly religious feel to them. It is not surprising to learn that his two great artistic heroes were Goya and Rembrandt, both of whose works were inbued with a sense of the suffering of life, and Rembrandt with his passionate faith. Amongst modern painters, his hero was Cézanne who also, incidentally, was a devout Catholic, attending Mass daily.

In paintings where the face is always powerful, Rouault painted clowns and judges. The intensity of feeling in a face is usually highlighted by some contrast with the clothing. In his paintings of clowns, for example, the clothing can be bright, even garish but we are caught by the haunting individuality and isolation of the face. As he wrote to a friend in 1905, when he describes seeing an old clown sitting in the corner of his wagon mending his striped, spangled costume:

> I saw clearly that the 'Clown' was myself, it was all of us (or almost all). The rich, spangled garment is given to us all to wear, and we are all clowns to a certain extent, we all wear 'Spangled garments', but if someone glimpses us unawares (as I glimpsed the old clown), oh! who can truthfully claim not to be moved to the very depths of his soul by enormous pity. My fault (if it is a fault, at any rate it causes me untold suffering) is *never to leave anyone their spangled garb*, be he king or emperor. It is the soul of the person standing in front of me that I want to see ... and the greater the person, the more extolled he is as a human being, the more I fear for the good of his soul.[70]

'*Who wears no disguise?*' was a title he used for a number of his paintings.

Rouault's sense of outrage at the cruelty of life was accompanied by a profound sympathy for those who suffered. Like Goya, he combined violence and pity, together with a faith which suffused them both. The result is that his paintings for all their sombre quality have gentleness in them. As has been well put: 'While he was only one of many painters of his time who chose to express themselves in violently expressive images, he was one of the very few who had the confidence to tread delicately.'[71]

Rouault had a huge output of paintings, most of them unfinished. But amongst the paintings he did finish were a good number on the theme of Christ. Amongst his famous images are those of Christ mocked and the head of Christ, a powerful picture full of intense agony. He gave one of his paintings a quotation from the French philosopher Pascal, 'Christ suffers until the end of the world.' Like so many twentieth-century poets, writers and theologians, Rouault's understanding of God is that he is above all one who shares in the suffering of humanity through Christ.[72]

In one of Rouault's crucifixion scenes, painted around 1920, the dark is once again a fundamental feature. The Crucifixion could almost be taking place at night. The sky is dark, the land is dark and the outline of the Cross is black. This serves to focus the eye of the viewer on the unearthly light of Christ's body and the faces of those by the Cross. The one shown here however, has streaks of light in the sky and all the figures are illuminated. The sky also has red in it. This could indicate sunset. A sunset might indicate the life of Christ going down into the darkness of death, but with the red holding out hope of the 'delights' to come (Red sky at night, Shepherd's delight). Or, on the other hand, if this is sunrise, this is a prefiguring of the dawn of Easter morning, without forgetting the death of Christ as a judgement on the world (Red sky in the morning, Shepherd's warning). Although the sky is streaked with light the figures are in fact lit from the front, from behind the viewer. It is from that light that the faces of the three figures beside the cross and the figure of Christ on it are lit up. In contrast to the 1920 painting described above, this greater light expresses a serene hope and joy.

The figures on either side of the Cross are absorbed in Christ's suffering in their own way. To the right, John raises his neck and face ardently in the directon of Jesus. Beside him, Mary the mother of Jesus, in her traditional blue, bends her head in sorrow. To the left, another figure, perhaps Mary Magdalene, kneels in devout prayer. The intention of these three figures helps to draw the onlooker into the picture and to make their own response. The head of Jesus, slightly on one side, with the eyes half closed, looks down gently and questioningly at the onlooker. This is not just a painting for public art, to be viewed from afar. It is the artist's deeply felt personal response to the Crucifixion which in turn seems to require a personal response from the viewer.

Figure 28: *The Crucifixion* by Stanley Spencer

The Crucifixion

— Stanley Spencer —

Great Britain has produced a number of religious artists that do not fit easily into any recognisable category, artistic or religious, for example, William Blake, and in the twentieth century, Eric Gill. Stanley Spencer was one of these. His paintings contained themes and images that were very personal to him. Many of these derived from happy childhood memories, but his paintings also have a wider significance because they touch on universal themes and often use traditional Christian imagery, albeit in a fresh way. Throughout his life, he painted scenes from the Passion cycle and just before the Second World War he began a remarkable series of paintings on Christ in the Wilderness, now in the Gallery of Western Australia, in Perth. The theme of Resurrection is also a major one for Spencer, perhaps the major one. For him, the Resurrection it is very much one to this life, with all its joys and sensual pleasures. This is true both of his later paintings, depicting people rising out of their graves in Cookham churchyard, as it is of his great *Resurrection of the Battlefield* in the Sandham Memorial Chapel at Burghclere near the Hampshire and Berkshire border. But because this book is primarily focused on the Crucifixion, it is that scene that has been illustrated here, rather than one of Spencer's Resurrection paintings.

Spencer was a consciously religious painter, who expressed his religion in a celebration of earthly things, however mundane. He believed that love, rooted in this religious feeling, was what made art possible: 'Love is the essential power in the creation of art and love is not a talent. Love reveals and more accurately describes the nature and meaning of things than any mere lecture on technique can do. It establishes once and for all time the final and perfect *identity* of every created thing.'[73]

For Spencer, this love was integrally intertwined with strong feelings of sexual attraction. In his paintings, he wants to affirm life and everything in it, not just the obviously beautiful, but the earthly and indeed what appears to many as the grotesque, all with one joyous, peaceful celebration.

In the light of this, it is therefore somewhat surprising that Spencer's final painting should be so stark and uncompromising in the human cruelty depicted. Spencer hated suffering and any dwelling on it in art. Yet this Crucifixion scene brings us up against some of the harshest aspects of human nature. But Spencer knew what he was doing. When there was a public outcry against the gleeful cruelty of the tormentors he was unabashed. The painting had been commissioned for Aldenham School. When he was invited to speak to the boys he said, 'It is your governors, and you, who are still nailing Christ to the Cross.' He knew that all of us have a capacity for human cruelty.[74]

The scene is set, as so often, in Cookham in Berkshire, this time in the middle of the High Street. Familiar houses are on either side but in the middle is a huge pile of rubble in which the crosses have been set. Spectators lean forward from the window of a house on the right, their faces full of the usual inquisitive curiosity. Spread on top of the mound is the prostrate figure of the Virgin Mary spread-eagled as though left there by the sea. The men who nail Christ to the Cross take a horrible pleasure in their task while one of the thieves strains forward to 'Cast the same in his teeth'. A schoolboy with disproportionately long legs ties the thief's arm to the crossbeam.

The City Livery Company that supports Aldenham School is based on the brewing trade. The two men hammering in the nails are depicted as brewers' men, in their distinctive hats. With their mouths full of nails they raise their hammers high above their heads and hold Christ's arms steady as they prepare to hit the nails home with all the force they can muster. At the top of the canvas, storm clouds gather. At the centre of all this terrible cruelty, Christ looks up to Heaven awaiting his fate.

This is a disturbing painting. But the Crucifixion of Christ, like all expressions of human cruelty, is rightly disturbing. One of the problems of painting the Crucifixion is that it can be turned into such a beautiful work of art that we lose any sense of its reality. The reality was as painful a form of torture as human ingenuity has devised. And this, sadly, is what human beings are still capable of.

Figure 29: *Noli Me Tangere* **by Graham Sutherland**

The *Noli Me Tangere*

— Graham Sutherland —

In the discussion of Giotto's fresco on the appearance of the risen Christ to
Mary Magdalene (see p. 73), the history of the depiction of the Noli Me
Tangere theme was briefly considered. It was never a key image for the
Church in the East, because of the tradition of the first appearance to Mary
the Mother of Christ. It was she who needed to be given pre-eminence, so
the appearance of Mary Magdalene was not singled out as a separate scene.

In the mediaeval West however, through the growing influence of the cult
of Mary Magdalene, the Noli Me Tangere scene came into prominence.
Examples include fine Romanesque reliefs in stone and bronze, illuminated
manuscripts such as the one in Lambeth Palace and, from the beginning of
the fourteenth century, a painting by Duccio on the back of his famous
Maesta in Sienna.[75] Renaissance painters after Giotto himself loved the
scene and there are fine paintings by Orcagna, Titian and others. The
tradition never completely died out: in 1771, for example, All Souls College,
Oxford placed in its chapel a painting of this scene which they had specially
commissioned from German artist Anton Raphael Mengs, painter to the
Court in Spain.

In the East, as the result of Western influence, the scene began to gain in
popularity, occuring in the Western-influenced mosaics in Monreale in
Sicily in the twelfth century. Then, after the Fall of Constantinople, when
icon painters escaped to Crete, Damaskinos painted the scene as did
Emmanuel Tzanes in 1657 for a church in Corfu. The scene occurs in at least
two churches in Cyprus from the last part of the fifteenth century.

From our own time, there is a sensitive sculpture in the garden of
Magdalen College, Oxford by David Wynn, but the best-known rendering is
the painting by Graham Sutherland commissioned by Dean Walter Hussey
for Chichester Cathedral.

Before looking more closely at the Sutherland painting it is important to
consider the meaning of this scene in the fourth Gospel. According to John:
'Jesus said to Mary, "Do not hold on to me, because I have not yet ascended

to the Father. But go to my brothers and say to them, 'I am ascending to my Father and your Father, to my God and your God''' (John 20:17).

What is meant by the phrase 'Do not hold on to me, because I have not *yet* ascended to the Father'? The presence of the word 'yet' indicates that Mary is not wrong in wanting to hold Christ close to her but that now is not the time when she is able to do that. The most satisfactory understanding of the verse sees it in relation to promises made earlier in the Gospel that after his resurrection Christ will be with his disciples as an abiding spiritual presence. It is in this sense that Mary will be able to 'hold' Christ. He will be close to her and the other disciples and they will enjoy his presence forever. No one will be able to take their joy from them. However, in the garden, in the transition from mortality to immortality, is not the time for this. Christ is ascending to his Father, who is also the God and Father of his disciples. It is this ascension which makes possible Christ's permanent in-dwelling of his disciples.

When we look at the Sutherland portrayal of this scene, the eye is drawn first to the great spaces of colour, the ochre/orange and the blue, especially the former. The spaces are square and somewhat severe blocks; this is 1960s architecture, albeit in a Mediterranean ambience. There is no attempt here at a visual re-creation of Palestine 2000 years ago. The background is twentieth-century southern France, or Spain.

The severity of the squares and sharp, concrete diagonals of the stairs serve to accentuate the bends and folds of the two figures. Indeed so bent is Christ that he is almost hunchback. Similarly Mary Magdalene is so folded over that she looks physically uncomfortable. But the rounded shoulders of Christ and the rounded bottom and breasts of Mary, together with the gentle curves of Christ's knee and Mary's neck emphasise the warm and human, in contrast to the impersonal and angular of the architecture. Here is a human meeting.

In this meeting there is a tenderness and intimacy. Christ looks gently down and reaches out to Mary who is looking up to him with pleading eyes. But all this is set, as if it were staged, on an outside staircase which Christ is ascending.

The meaning of the story in John, as already mentioned, is that Mary is not to cling to Christ in his present, physical form. His promise that he will be with his followers forever, is to be fulfilled in a spiritual manner. When he has ascended, then he will be close to them in an abiding, spiritual way. This scene, in a brilliant manner, depicts a moment which is at once one of intimacy and withdrawal. Mary reaches out in a desperate longing to touch and grasp the risen Christ. Jesus bends over, towards us, looking down and reaching out with a look and gesture of intimate meeting. However, Christ is ascending the steps: his elongated body and leg, with foot dragging on the ground at the bottom of the stairs, his arms along the banister, finger pointing heavenwards, indicate a movement towards the heavenly.

Yet his Heaven is not just 'up there'. The azure sky can also be seen, as it were, through the building. The ochre of the building and the blue sky (Heaven) are not simply set one against the other. 'We can look through earth to see heaven in our midst', as well as up above. Christ, set against the sky behind the building, could just as much merge into and emerge from that as shoot into the heavens. Indeed, the palms behind him are almost rays of light, and the whole scene is bathed in the bright sunlight of eternity.

Christ in his old gardener's hat has come amongst us as a human being; a little keyhole at the bottom left of the picture could indicate the one through whom we see God.

Christ meets Mary in moment of intimate recognition. But this intimacy is at the same time his moment of withdrawal into Heaven – behind, beyond and within all things. He disappears into that background in order that he might be in our foreground in a new way: a spiritual presence in our hearts and minds.

Figure 30: *Supper at Emmaus* **by Ceri Richards**

The *Supper at Emmaus*

— Ceri Richards —

The story of the appearance of the risen Christ to two disciples falls into two parts. First, there is the actual journey on the road to Emmaus, when Christ expounded the Hebrew Scriptures to them. The moment as evening was falling when the disciples invite the stranger to stay with them was depicted in a mediaeval relief in Autun Cathedral, which was described earlier (see p. 57). The second part of the story concerns the actual Supper, particularly the moment when the two disciples recognise the stranger to be Christ. At the time of the Counter-Reformation, when the Eucharist became subject to renewed attention, this scene became particularly popular amongst Christian artists. A very striking rendering by Caravaggio has already been shown (see p. 97). A modern rendering, by Ceri Richards, is no less striking.

Commissioned in 1958 by the Junior Common Room of St Edmund College, Oxford, as part of a competition amongst major artists of the time, it was put in the Chapel to celebrate the transition of the Hall to a recognised college of the University. It was well received at the time, receiving good reviews in both *The Sunday Times* and *The Observer*, and it continues to arouse appreciation.

Luke records that 'Their eyes were opened and they recognised him; and he vanished out of their sight' (24:31). This moment of recognition was most dramatically caught by Caravaggio in his great shaft of light across the picture and the startled faces of the disciples. In Ceri Richards's portrayal, Christ is seated against a great yellow cross of light which at once outlines him and allows him to melt into it. Richards was also responsible for the design of the Sacrament Chapel in the Roman Catholic Cathedral in Liverpool. There, both in the painting behind the altar and in the stained-glass window, yellow light plays a crucial role. Here the light is not shining on Christ but is behind him forming the background out of which he emerges – the light of eternity in which he is momentarily figured as a human face and form.

The two disciples react to the revelation of Christ in different ways. One rises awkwardly, pushing the chair aside. The other, seated at the side of the table is 'disturbed but uncomprehending; his clasped hands are pressed to his mouth in the gesture of a slow man gaining time to readjust his mind'.[76] It is a powerful icon in which the sudden apprehension of one disciple and the delayed recognition of the other are juxtaposed.

The most unusual feature of the painting, however, is the large hands and feet of both the disciples and Christ himself. Narrowed wrists and ankles make them unusually prominent. Big feet featured in Stanley Spencer's *Last Supper* of 1920, now at Cookham, as later in Picasso's 1930 *Crucifixion* and his *Guernica*. But Richards is doing more than sharing in an iconographic fad. The prominence of the hands and feet bring to mind a prayer attributed to St Teresa of Avila:

> Christ has no body now on earth but ours,
> No hands but ours,
> No feet but ours,
> Ours the eyes through which he is to look Christ's compassion to the world;
> Ours are the feet with which he is to go about doing good.
> Ours are the hands with which he is to bless men now.

Hands and feet provide these specific, practical means of doing good. The moment of recognition of the risen Christ is also the moment of realisation that his work continues through human hands and feet. The hand that raised to bless and teach is a hand that will henceforth work through those large, ungainly yet beautiful extremities of flesh and blood: 'It is the imaginative, centrifugal movement of the hands and feet that serves to interrelate the figures and gives them a buoyancy half suggestive of resurrection.'[77] Christ in his risen body gives his disciples the blessed bread, his body broken for humanity, that they might become his risen body in the world.

Figure 31: *Crucifixion* **by Helen Meyer**

'A Sword Shall Pierce through Thy Own Soul'

— *Crucifixion* by Helen Meyer —

In 1981 I made a television programme with Helen Meyer based on a new set of stations of the cross which she had recently painted. We focused on each scene in turn, both talking about what we discerned in the painting. This depiction of Christ on the cross is traditionally the twelfth station in what eventually became standardised as fourteen stations.

The devotion known as the stations of the cross originated with the Franciscans in the Holy Land in the thirteenth century. Originally it took the form of physically visiting and praying at the different sites in Jerusalem associated with the final week in the life of Jesus. In due course, due to popular demand, these stations were reproduced for churches all over Europe and, as mentioned above, were fixed at fourteen. They were designed to facilitate the intense personal piety which the Franciscans set out to encourage. The pilgrim or worshiper was exhorted to imagine themselves actually there at the particular point where Jesus fell, or was flagellated, feeling the appropriate emotions. So, in many churches the separate scenes are set around the walls, together with a cross at each point, and people are encouraged, especially during Holy Week, to stop at each station and pray. Most sets of stations of the cross are of course designed simply to be aids to devotion and they do not claim to be works of art. Nevertheless some works of art have come about in this way, for example the set by Tiepolo in Venice, by Eric Gill in Westminster Cathedral, and in our own time, Norman Adams in Manchester.

Helen Meyer trained at both the Camberwell and Edinburgh colleges of art. Her main work continues to be sculpture and wood carving but she continues to combine this with some painting. This crucifixion in its simplicity and concentration on essentials reflects the standard iconography of the eastern tradition, with Jesus on the cross and just two figures either side, John and Mary. But the artistic influences behind it are Romanesque art and the work of Giotto.

Mary has her traditional blue head covering but her dress and the clothing of John are a more unusual sombre purple; not the purple of royalty but of mourning. These two figures are not standing apart from the cross as in traditional depictions but close to it, with their hands on the body of Jesus, on his stomach and chest as though trying to offer comfort. There is sadness and pity in their faces as there is sadness and pity in the face of Jesus looking down upon them. His body, particularly the arms, are thin, with a sense of fragility and gentleness.

Helen Meyer has said that in the painting of this scene the words of Simeon to Mary, when the child Jesus was brought to the temple, kept coming into her mind. Mary is told that the child was set 'For the fall and rising again of many in Israel' and that 'A sword shall pierce through thy own soul also'. (Luke 2: 35) This crucifixion captures well that pain of Mary, the piercing of the heart and the searing of the soul at the cruel death of Jesus. Like any mother she seeks to touch, gently hold and comfort her beloved son.

It is true of many artists that sometimes deep experiences from their personal life imbue a particular painting of a historical scene with a special feeling or mood. Stanley Spencer, for example, made it almost a point of principle to incorporate the feelings he had as a child into his painting of the gospel scenes. Helen Meyer's brother was killed in the invasion of France near Caen in 1944 where he fought with the Highland Regiment, when he was 22 and she was 14. This sad loss of her beloved brother has remained with her ever since, and surfaced very strongly when she was painting this particular scene.

The painting conveys a sense of isolation in a strange and spacious landscape, somewhat in the manner of Cragie Aitcheson. The light coming from the front means that the cross and the figures cast shadows on the ground, shadows which point to the dark line of the hills in the background. The shadows and the dark outline suggest the sombre nature of our human reality, as does the dark black outline of the cross itself. All is however set against a large expanse of sky in luminous red. This startling red, a feature of all Helen Meyer's stations of the cross, is ambiguous and complex in its effects. It is at once the blood red of torture and agony: but also a red that is luminous with something else. It is a sky red from a great blaze behind the hills; a sky lit up in brilliant red as the sun sinks down below the horizon; a red which is at once the anguish of the world and the glory of God. But the glory of God is above all in the intense emotion captured by the gestures and faces of the three figures, in the sheer pity, the pity of John and Mary for their beloved Jesus, the pity of Jesus for the plight of humanity. This is a painting of intense feeling and faith, conveying as it does both the soul of Mary pierced through and the soul of Jesus pierced through for his love of humanity.

Figure 32: *Menorah* by Roger Wagner

Menorah

— Roger Wagner —

Roger Wagner, who was born in 1957, stands in the tradition of Samuel Palmer, the nineteenth-century visionary landscape painter. From a literary point of view he brings to mind Thomas Traherne, with his childhood awareness of all things shimmering with the divine. At the same time, Wagner's paintings have a Christian symbolism that challenges our complacent liberalism. For example, his stunning painting of a field of wheat, which perfectly visualises Traherne's 'Orient and immortal wheat', depicts angels reaping with scythes and bears the title *Harvest is the end of the world, and the reapers are angels*.

Roger Wagner often works on a small scale for, as he has said, 'Too many large paintings are just inflated small ones.'[78] When he works on a large scale, as here (the painting is roughly 1.5 metres by 2 metres) it is because a number of different elements have come together forcing, of natural necessity, large scale. One element is the view of Didcot Power Station, another may be Paul Nash's wartime landscapes with their devastated woods. Another is a photograph taken in the Crimea in 1942, which shows women looking for their loved ones among the bodies which lie strewn across a smoke-filled landscape.[79]

Wagner's original version was of a deposition in front of the Didcot Power Station cooling towers, with the figures attending Christ dressed in the striped uniform of the death camps and carrying the yellow Star of David. It was later that the chimneys evoked the idea of the Menorah, the Jewish symbol for the presence of God. As with his other paintings, Wagner brings together disparate elements, from different historical periods, into an aesthetic whole which is visually fresh and morally challenging. The cooling towers of Didcot Power Station dominate the landscape for twenty or more miles round Oxfordshire and the former West Berkshire. Though obtrusive they are not unbeautiful. In an association that is at once striking and dangerous, Wagner sees them as both the gas ovens of the Nazi extermination programme and the Jewish Menorah, the seven-branched candlestick which gives its name to the picture.

In the foreground are figures that are recognisably Jewish without being stereotypical. They convey an impression of utter, abject grief. To the left, a man, staring in horror, comforts his wife. One man hides his head and bends low, unable to look anywhere; two others cover their faces with their hands. A woman looks away while she and the man next to her hold out their arms in anger and dismay. The sense of impotence and despair make them speechless.

Wagner sees in nature a luminous numinosity, as in his paintings of trees. But he is no pastoral escapist. Here, and in his studies of the Menorah, he confronts the most shocking of the many moral outrages of the so-called advanced twentieth century, the *Shoah*.

Across the painting, in the middle ground, are three crucified figures; the central figure, with an inscription above his head, is clearly the Jesus of Christian iconography. What is Wagner saying? These are victims, Jewish victims, of State power: victims belong together whether killed by the Romans or the Nazis. Four figures gather round the Cross in the centre, three of them lifting their arms and pointing. The pointing could be accusatory, for the Cross has too often been used as an instrument of anti-Judaism, to bludgeon psychologically (and sometimes physically) the Jewish people. But Wagner is a devout Christian, so there will be more in this gesture than an accusation. For Christian believers, the Crucifixion is a sign that God suffers in all human suffering and especially this must be true of the suffering of his chosen people.

As was pointed out in considering Chagall's *White Crucifixion*, Christians need to tread with fear and trepidation when they associate the Crucifixion of Jesus with Jewish suffering. Chagall was a Jew, Wagner is a Christian. But this picture does not, I think, in any way lessen the impact of the *Shoah* or take away from the reality of Jewish suffering. On the contrary it reveals unspeakable, bleak desolation. When Jesus cries out from the Cross, it is as a Jew to a Jewish God, who is also the God who loves all people.

The light in Wagner's paintings is always distinctive, almost surreal, and this is certainly so here. It could be the first light of dawn or the light of evening, yet the effect is somehow starker than that. It is nothing less than the light of judgement, revealing all things with terrible, searing clarity. The light on the flooded loam, shining on the clay, gives the landscape a bleak, unearthly feel. The reflection of the giant cooling towers in the water almost overwhelm. Light, because it is God's light, uncreated and created, can never be without hope, so the light on the towers, even the light on the clouds of steam/smoke presages something better. The presence of the Menorah indicates that even in the death camps, so many Jews sought to be faithful to the one who seemed to have abandoned them. For Christians, God is also here, in the Cross. But this hope, if it is received as such, cannot be seen apart from the light that lays everything bare, the terrible cruelty, the unspeakable grief.

Figure 33: *The Incredulity of Thomas* **by Nicholas Mynheer**

The Incredulity of Thomas

— Nicholas Mynheer —

Illustrated in an earlier section was a Byzantine mosaic of the appearance of the risen Christ to Thomas (see p. 33). This scene was familiar in the West and appeared, for example, in the other half of the Chairete mosaic in Venice in the twelfth century (see p. 61). From the same century there is a carved stone relief at Silos in Spain on the pilgrimage route. Around 1600, Caravaggio painted the scene in a way that contempories found irreverent and even outrageous: the apostles, instead of being painted as beautiful figures, looked like common labourers with weathered faces and wrinkled brows. Thomas is shown thrusting his finger into Christ's side in a very vigorous, physical manner. Surprisingly, in our own century of doubt, there is a paucity of paintings on this theme.

In 1991 Nicholas Mynheer painted a series of paintings, The Way of the Cross, for St Matthew's Church in Perry Beeches, Birmingham.[80] He felt his series was incomplete without taking into account the truth of the Resurrection, so he painted four Resurrection scenes, one of which is illustrated here. All four scenes have backgrounds of gold, conveying the light and glory of the new order of which the Resurrection of Christ is an anticipation.

After training at Hornsey Art College, Nicholas Mynheer (born in 1958) worked originally in advertising. Following his conversion to Christianity, through the influence of his wife, he turned full-time to painting, which he has done now for nearly two decades, his style evolving all the time. One strong characteristic of his current style is his desire to concentrate on the essential features and feeling of a scene, cutting out all extraneous detail. This has produced his characteristic figures, with their large elongated heads and huge hands. His strong, flowing lines, together with powerful blocks of colour make his paintings both vivid and accessible. At times, these qualities give his pictures a medieval flavour like stained glass or even cloisonné. An even more marked feature of his painting is the way the face of Christ bends over the figures, as illustrated here. This, together with flowing lines, conveys a moving sense of the compassion of Christ enfolding the figures before him.

Three disciples are shown, with Thomas in the middle in red. All are wide-eyed and open-mouthed with amazement. Thomas lifts his left arm and points to the wound in Christ's side with his hand. There is astonishment and wonder which, as we know from the Gospel account, leads on to Thomas's profession of faith, 'My Lord and God' (John 20:28).

Christ holds out his large hands, with palms facing us to reveal his wounds. The openness of these wounded hands, together with Christ gently and lovingly encompassing the figures with his arms is a wonderful icon for our doubting times. Whatever our questions and objections, the wounded love of God enfolds us.

Notes

[1] For an analysis of the different phases of catacomb painting, see L. V. Rutgers, *Subterranean Rome*, Peeters, 2000.

[2] For a helpful discussion of the different symbols, images and narratives see Robin Margaret Jenson, *Understanding Early Christian Art*, Routledge, 2000.

[3] Antonio Ferrua, *The Unknown Catacomb*, Geddes and Grosset, 1991, p. 15.

[4] Fabrizio Marcinelli, *Catacombs and Basilicas*, Scala, Florence, 1981, p. 27.

[5] Gertrud Schiller, *Icnography of Christian Art, Vol. 2, The Passion of Jesus Christ*, Lund Humphries, 1972, p. 5; cited as *Iconography of Christian Art*.

[6] Thomas Mathews, *The Clash of Gods, A Reinterpretation of Christian Art*, Princeton University Press, 1993, pp. 157–64.

[7] For examples on coinage see *The Image of Christ*, The National Gallery, 2000, figs 6 and 8.

[8] See Jas Elsner, *Art and the Roman Viewer: The Transformation of Art from the Pagan World to Christianity*, Cambridge University Press, 1995, and Jas Elsner, *Imperial Rome and Christian Triumph: The Art of the Roman Empire AD 100–450*, Oxford University Press, 1998.

[9] See *The Image of Christ*, Section 43.

[10] For a discussion of the lateness of the emergence of this image see Jenson, *Understanding Early Christian Art*, Chapter 5.

[11] Nigel Spivey, *Enduring Creation: Art, Pain and Fortitude*, Thames and Hudson, 2001, p. 33.

[12] For the development of the rotunda see Martin Biddle, *The Tomb of Christ*, Sutton, 1999.

[13] Anna Kartsonis, *Anastasis, The Making of an Image*, Princeton University Press, 1986, p. 25; cited as *Anastasis*.

[14] Andre Grabar, *Christian Iconography, A Study of its Origins*, Princeton University Press, 1968, p. 124; cited as *Christian Iconography*.

[15] Robin Cormack, *Byzantine Art*, Oxford University Press, 2000, pp. 68–71.

[16] A. and J. Stylianou, 'By this Conquer', *Publications of the Society of Cypriote Studies*, No. 4, Nicosia, Cyprus, 1971.

[17] On Irish crosses, see Hilary Richardson and John Scarry, *An Introduction to Irish High Crosses*, Mercier Press, 1990. For Scotland, see Sally M. Foster, Picts, Gaels and Scots, Batsford, 1997, Chapter 5.

[18] Hilary Richardson, 'The Jewelled Cross and its Canopy', in *From the Isles of the North*, ed. Cormac Bourke, HMSO, 1995.

[19] Vrej Nersessian, *Treasures from the Ark, 1700 Years of Armenian Christian Art*, The British Library, 2001, pp. 110–12.

[20] Kartsonis, *Anastasis*, Chapter 3.

[21] John Beckwith, *Early Christian and Byzantine Art*, Penguin, 1979, p. 230.

²² *Medieval Cloisonne Enamels*, Georgian State Museum of Fine Arts, 1984, figs 1, 12 and 31.

²³ Cormack, *Byzantine Art*, p. 167.

²⁴ The Acts of Paul and Thekla, trans. J. K. Elliot, in *The Apocryphal New Testament*, Oxford University Press, 1993, pp. 364–80.

²⁵ The Gospel of Nicodemus, trans. Elliott, *Apocryphal New Testament*, pp. 164–204.

²⁶ This is the view of Kartsonis in *Anastasis*. Her book is the most detailed and comprehensive study of the emergence of this image.

²⁷ Grabar, *Christian Iconography*, p. 126.

²⁸ *The Medieval Treasury, The Art of the Middle Ages in the Victoria and Albert Museum*, ed. Paul Williamson, V&A Museum, 1986, p. 70. See also John Beckwith, *Early Medieval Art*, Thames and Hudson, 1969, pp. 65ff.

²⁹ Henry Mayr-Harting, *Ottonian Book Illumination*, Vol. 1, Oxford University Press, 1991, pp. 126ff.

³⁰ *Chronicle of Thietmar of Merseberg*, ed. Robert Holtzmann, *Monuments Germaniae Historica*, Berlin, 1995, Book iii, Chapter 2, pp. 98–101. There is a translation, with a discussion, in Henry Mayr-Harting, *Ottonian Book Illumination: An Historical Study*, Harvey Miller, 1991, Vol. i, p. 134.

³¹ *Guia Visual Art Romanic*, National Museum of Catalan Art, Barcelona, 2002, Chapter 12. Also *Romanesque Art Guide*, National Museum of Catalan Art, Second Edition, 2000, pp. 115–17.

³² *Il Volto di Christo*, Electa, Milan, 2000, figure vi.i and p. 271.

³³ For some examples see *English Romanesque Art, 1066–1200*, Arts Council, 1984, pp. 239–47.

³⁴ Schiller, *Iconography of Christian Art*, p. 145.

³⁵ Andreas and Judith Stylianou, *The Painted Churches of Cyprus*, Trigograph, 1985, p. 409.

³⁶ Brian Young, *The Villein's Bible*, Barrie and Jenkins, 1990, p. 117.

³⁷ Cyril Margo, *The Art of the Byzantine Empire*, University of Toronto Press, 1986, p. 68.

³⁸ Otto Demus, *The Mosaic Decoration of San Marco*, Venice, University of Chicago Press, 1988, p. 74.

³⁹ St Romanos, *On the Life of Christ, Kontakia*, trans. Ephrem Lash, HarperCollins, 1995, p. 148.

⁴⁰ R. W. Southern, *The Making of the Middle Ages*, Pimlico, 1993, p. 221ff.

⁴¹ C. E. Pocknee, *Cross and Crucifix*, Mowbrays, 1962, p. 48.

⁴² *Age of Chilvalry*, eds Jonathan Alexander and Paul Biniski, Royal Academy of Arts, 1987, p. 331.

⁴³ Monica Chiellini, *Cimabue*, Scala, 1988, p. 8.

⁴⁴ See Anne Derbes, *Picturing the Passion in Late Mediaeval Italy: Narrative Painting, Franciscan Ideologies and the Levant*, Cambridge University Press, 1998.

⁴⁵ Henk van Os, *Sienese Altar Pieces 1215–1460*, Egbert Forsten, 1988, p. 51.

⁴⁶ For a plan of the sequence see Bruce Cole, *Giotto, The Scrovengi Chapel, Padua*, George Braziller, 1993, p. 26.

⁴⁷ Moshe Barasch, *Giotto and the Language of Gesture*, Cambridge University Press, 1990, pp. 169ff.

⁴⁸ *The Golden Legend*, New York, 1969, p. 221.

⁴⁹ Augustine, *City of God*, XI.18.

⁵⁰ I am grateful to an unpublished paper by Mary Rogers for information in this paragraph.

⁵¹ Kartsonis, *Anastasis*, p. 213.

⁵² Ibid., pp. 212–13.

⁵³ Henk van Os, *The Art of Devotion*, Merrell Holberton, 1994, based on the exhibition at the Rijksmuseum, Amsterdam in 1995, p. 110.

⁵⁴ Ibid.

⁵⁵ *The Image of Christ*, section 44.

⁵⁶ Schiller, *Iconography of Christian Art*, p. 198.

⁵⁷ Carlo Bertelli, *Piero della Francesca*, Yale University Press, 1992, p. 198.

⁵⁸ Aldous Huxley, 'The Best Picture' in *Along the Road*, Flamingo Modern Classic, 1994, p. 109.

⁵⁹ Ann Stieghlitz, 'The Reproduction of Agony: toward a reception-history of Grunewald's Isenheim Altar after the First World War', *The Oxford Art Journal*, 12:2, 1989.

⁶⁰ Jane Dillenberger, *Style and Content in Christian Art*, SCM, 1965, pp. 143ff.

⁶¹ For a description see Helen de Borchgrave, *A Journey into Christian Art*, Lion, 1999, pp. 96.

⁶² John Drury, *Painting the Word: Christian Pictures and their Meanings*, National Gallery, 1999, p. 125.

⁶³ Ibid., pp. 127–8.

⁶⁴ Hidde Hockstna, *Rembrandt and the Bible*, Magna Books, 1990, p. 396.

⁶⁵ Hugh Honour, *Romanticism*, Penguin, 1991, p. 77.

⁶⁶ Joseph Leo Koerner, *Caspar David Friedrich and the Subject of Landscape*, Reaktion Books, 1990, Part II.

⁶⁷ Michel Makarius, *Chagall*, Studio Editions, 1988, p. 13.

⁶⁸ Royal Academy of Arts, London, 1985 Exhibition Catalogue, *Chagall*, pp. 16–19, 214.

⁶⁹ Fabrice Hergott and Sarah Whitfield, *Georges Rouault*, Royal Academy of Arts, London, 1993.

⁷⁰ Cited in Georges Rouault, *Sur l'art et sur la vie*, Paris, 1971, p. 150.

⁷¹ Ibid., p. 21.

⁷² Jane Dillenberger, *Style and Content in Christian Art*, SCM, 1965, pp. 206ff.

⁷³ *Stanley Spencer – the Apotheosis of Love*, Barbican Art Gallery, 1991.

⁷⁴ Duncan Robinson, *Stanley Spencer*, Phaidon Press, 1990, p. 121.

⁷⁵ *Maesta*, meaning 'majesty', refers to a painting of Mary enthroned.

⁷⁶ J. R. Hale, quoted by J. N. D. Kelly in *The St Edmund Hall Magazine*, 1958–59.

⁷⁷ Neville Wallis, *The Observer*, 28 Dec. 1958.

⁷⁸ Rupert Martin, 'Roger Wagner's Visionary Landscapes', in *Image: A Journal of the Arts*.

⁷⁹ Christopher Miller, Leaflet for the 1994 Ashmolean Museum Exhibition.

⁸⁰ Reviewed in the *Church Times* by Richard Davey, 13 April 1995. A triptych on the theme of life, death and resurrection was made for Lady Margaret Hall, Oxford. It is pictured in *Church Building*, Autumn 1992, and discussed by Alan Doig, pp. 27–8.

Index

Cyprus 24, 57, 123

Damaskinos 123
Daniel 1
Daphni 33, 36,
    mosaic 39, 81
Day of the Atonement 110
dead, raised by Christ 37
Dean Walter Hussey 123
death 1–2, 11, 20, 30, 31, 90, 91
    liberation from 38
    the skull of 31
death camps 135, 136
deliverance, theme of 1, 13
devotion, religious xi, 61, 66, 67, 69, 73,
    85, 86
    aids to 131
Didcot Power Station 135
dignity 49, 51
Dillenberger, Jane 93
diptych 86
disciples 11, 57, 61, 97, 124, 127, 128, 140
Dominicans 69
Domitilla xiv, 2, 4, 5, 6, 7
door(s) 34
Dorchester Abbey 77
dove(s) 8, 50
drama 39
'Dream of the Rood' 25–6
Drury, John 97, 98
Duccio 70, 123
    Maesta 70
Dumbarton Oaks 16, 61
Dumfries 25
Dunkirk 102
Duns Scotus 77
Duomo in Siena 70
Duomo of Borgo Sansepolcro 54
Dura-Europos 15
Dürer 93

eagle, the 7
Easter 39, 117

Eastern Church 30
Ecclesia 44
Elijah 110
Emmaus
    Halt at 56
    the road to 57, 58, 127
    Supper at, (*The*) 96, 97 98, 126, 127
Emperor Augustus 49
Emperor Constantine 6, 7, 12, 16, 19, 23,
    26, 43
Emperor Heraclius 23
Emperor Jovian 6
Emperor Theodosius 12, 43
emperors, depiction of 38
empty tomb, the 6, 11, 15, 16, 17, 20, 33,
    74, 89
end of the world 69, 93
England 54
engraving(s) 85, 86
Epictetus 12
ergotism 93
Eucharist, the 44, 49, 86, 94, 95, 98, 127
Eusebius 6
Eve 37, 39, 81, 82
Exodus, the 111
Expressionist 115

face(s) 115–16, 117, 120, 127, 132
feet, large 128
First World War 94, 109
fish(es) xiv, 2
Florence 54, 69
foliage 26
France 48, 57, 77, 109, 124
Franciscan
    influence xi
    prayer book 85
Franciscans 67, 69, 70, 131
Freising 48, 50
fresco(es) 13, 19, 38, 57, 74, 81, 89
friars 67, 69
Friedrich, Caspar David 104, 105